AF402843

Martin Reén

ABIDING IN THE FATHER'S LOVE

The Glorious Freedom of Sons and Daughters

Proofreading: Marie Enoksson
Published by: Healing Streams
Print: BoD – Books on Demand, Norderstedt, Tyskland
ISBN: 978-91-527-3596-1

TABLE OF CONTENTS

PREFACE

Already while I was writing my first book, I knew that I needed to write this book as well. My first book, *Transformed by the Grace of God,* was all about knowing the transforming power of God's grace and knowing our identity in Christ. Having an encounter with the grace of God inevitably leads to discovering the love of the Father. This book basically consists of the truths I learned on my personal journey of discovering His love. This was a journey that took me from living as an orphan, to finding my home in the Father's heart and embracing my identity as a son of God. When I was born again and Jesus came into my life, I had such a longing to serve Him and to lay down my life for His cause. This longing had been placed in my heart by God, but because I still lived with Him as an orphan, this longing was mixed with a lot of legalistic striving to please God.

Throughout my journey with God, my revelation of His love was growing and I began to realize who He really is. This became my process of getting to know God as my Father. This process is not over yet and I'm still coming to know Him in a deeper and more intimate way. As I got to know God as my Father, I also realized that I am His beloved son and that He is well pleased with me. That revelation has healed my heart and led me into a life of rest and freedom. I still want to please God and lay down my life for the gospel, but the motivation for doing so is different. Before, I was always looking for the approval of God and to earn a place at His table. Now I know that I have His approval and that I have always had a big place in His heart. So, like Paul I am now living with the motivation that *"the love of Christ compels us, because we judge thus: that if One died for all, then all died; and He died for all, that those who live should live no longer for themselves, but for Him who died for them and rose again"* (2 Cor. 5:14-15).

Throughout the pages of this book, I want to share some of the insights and revelations that has strengthened and encouraged me throughout my journey. My hope and prayer are for you to get to know the heart of the Father in deeper ways, and for you to start to live out of your identity as His child, enjoying the full benefits of all the blessings that you now have received in Christ. Hopefully, this book will both inspire and encourage you on the journey into the heart of the Father.

Your brother in Christ,
Martin Reén

INTRODUCTION

And we have known and believed the love that God has for us. God is love, and he who abides in love abides in God, and God in him. Love has been perfected among us in this: that we may have boldness in the day of judgment; because as He is, so are we in this world. There is no fear in love; but perfect love casts out fear, because fear involves torment. But he who fears has not been made perfect in love. We love Him because He first loved us (1 John 4:16-19 NKJV).

In my first book, *Transformed by The Grace of God*, I wrote about how the grace of God brings true transformation into our lives as believers. This book is building on the foundation I laid in that book. I have written this book to reveal the love of the Father and how abiding in His love establishes us in our new identity, both as individual believers and as His family. The Bible describes the life of sonship in such terms as the glorious liberty of the children of God. Therefore, I have chosen to call this book *Abiding in the Father's Love — The Glorious Freedom of Sons and Daughters*. This is the first book in a series on abiding in the love of God, where we study the depths of His love for us. The other books in this series are:

- *Partnering with the Love of Christ*
- *The Burning Love of Christ*
- *Sonship, Faith and Vision*

I highly recommend that you read those books as well. This is a series that is written to reveal the love of God, and each book will point to many different aspects of His great love. In this book, we will focus on how the love of the Father restores us into sonship and Christlikeness.

A Book about Our Freedom as Children of God

True freedom is found as we learn to abide in the Father's love, and His love delivers and restores us into becoming our true and most authentic selves. One of the key verses, which I have built this book upon is this one:

For the creation was subjected to frustration, not by its own choice, but by the will of the one who subjected it, in hope that the creation itself will be liberated from its bondage to decay and brought into the freedom and glory of the children of God (Rom. 8:20-21 NIV).

Paul describes our lives in terms of the freedom and glory of the children of God. This life of ever increasing freedom and glory is accessible to us as we grow in revelation of His great love for us. Our freedom as the children of God could be summarized in one word: Christlikeness.

Defining Christlikeness

It is important to understand the meaning of being Christlike and how this relates to the Father's deep longing to bring His people into His glorious freedom. To understand true freedom, we need to start by looking at Christ.

The Son is the radiance and only expression of the glory of [our awesome] God [reflecting God's Shekinah glory, the Light-being, the brilliant light of the divine], and the exact representation and perfect imprint of His [Father's] essence, and upholding and maintaining and propelling all things [the entire physical and spiritual universe] by His powerful word [carrying the universe along to its predetermined goal] (Hebr. 1:3 AMP).

Jesus is the perfect representation and image of the Father. When we look at Jesus, we see who the Father is, but not only does Jesus reveal the Father's true face. He reveals what it means to be fully human, without the damage of sin. Jesus is God's original picture and we have been created in His image (Eph. 2:10). Jesus is the second Adam and He is the head of a new humanity that consists of all the sons and daughters of God (1 Cor. 15:45-47). He is also the first man and the firstborn among many brethren (Rom. 8:29). In other words, if we want to live in the freedom of the children of God, we must start by looking at Christ.

If we try to find identity or freedom anywhere else than in Christ, we will always end up in confusion. That includes trying to find our identity by looking inside of ourselves. We have been created in the image of God, but because of sin and the influence of the world that image has been distorted. This is why we need to keep our eyes on Jesus, who is the original picture, if we want to find out what the Father had on His heart when He created us. This process that God brings us through to restore the image of Christ in us is what the Bible describes as the process of sanctification. That means that we are becoming who we already are. This is the only path to true freedom.

Becoming Christlike doesn't mean that we lose our personalities or become a pale copy of someone else. When we're growing into the image of Christ, we are being restored into our truest selves. Jesus Christ is big and no one could really reflect His fullness all by himself. So, there is no need to worry that you're becoming a boring copy of someone else, or that you will lose your dreams, passions and gifts. They have been placed there by God, so you will not lose them, but what will happen is that our personalities will be restored by the love of the Father, so that we can live out our dreams and our passions. We will begin to operate in all the gifts that God has given us in a pure way. That is true freedom! The Father loves us into wholeness, so that we can embrace life as the beautiful gift that it really is!

A Reflection of my Personal Journey in God

This book is in many ways the depiction of my personal journey, so I will be sharing some of my own experiences of encountering the love of the Father, throughout these pages. It has always been important for me to not preach, teach, or write information that I know through studies only. I want to share the revelations and insights that has transformed my life. One of the most important revelations I have ever received from heaven, must certainly be this one about abiding in the Father's love. His love has changed my life in more ways than I ever have thought possible. I am fully convinced that it is impossible to encounter the Father's love and remain the same. The Father's love is a transforming power that heals and restores every broken heart. I have written this book to share some of the insights that I have gained on my own journey into knowing God as my Father. To make it as easy as possible to follow my thoughts, I have divided this book into three parts:

- *Abiding in the Father's Love*

In the first part of this book, we will be looking at how we have been brought home to the Father. We will see how this revelation transforms our lives. We will also find out more about abiding in the love of God, the restoration of our sonship and childlikeness. These truths are the foundation of a life in freedom and sonship.

- *Restoration of the Whole Man*

In the second part, we will look at how our souls are restored by the love of the Father. Our mind is renewed, our will is set free and our emotions are healed by the power of the Father's love. We will study how His love brings healing to other areas of our life as well. We become who we were always meant to be, when we embrace our identity as His beloved children. His love heals our broken hearts and liberates us to become the people that He has called us to be.

- *From Bondage to Freedom*

In the third part, we will be looking at some of the areas that are impacted and transformed as we enter the glorious freedom that belongs to the children of God. I want to unveil something of the radical difference between the slavery of religion, compared to a life that has been liberated and restored by the Father's love. To abide in His love changes a lot of things in our lives.

The Activations

At the end of each chapter, there is a section called Activations. Within them you'll find simple activations that will help you to put the truths of this book into action. They are there to provide practical application to the teaching. You will get the most out of this book if you take time to do these activations. They will help you to interact with the Holy Spirit and gain more revelation on the topic presented within each chapter. They are very simple to work with and they will inspire you to grow in deeper intimacy with the Father. All these activations do involve journaling, so I suggest that you have a notebook or an electronic device within reach when reading this book. In the Kingdom of God, we learn best by applying revelation. These activations will be helpful and fun as you interact with the Holy Spirit.

I hope and pray that reading this book will be just as exciting and challenging for you, as it has been for me to write it. I hope that the revelation that you gain from reading these pages will build, strengthen, comfort, and encourage you along your journey into the Father's love. Deep calls unto deep on that journey and there is always more of His heart to explore. Let's dive deep into the heart of the Father to explore the transforming power of His love!

Part 1:

Abiding in the Father's Love

Behold, what manner of love the Father hath bestowed upon us, that we should be called the sons of God: therefore the world knoweth us not, because it knew him not (1 John 3:1).

God is our Father and we are His beloved and favored children. He is well pleased with us. Through Jesus Christ, He has brought us home, so that we have a place at His side forever. By doing so, He has given us a new identity, a home together with Him and a heavenly inheritance. In this part of the book, we will look at how we can grow in our revelation and insight about these glorious truths. The freedom and joy that we can experience as believers, are directly tied to us learning to abide in the love of the Father. As we're abiding in His unconditional approval and love, we'll find our home in His presence, where we are delivered from our identity as orphans. We will instead begin to be restored into our identity as His beloved children. In other words, this part of the book is about how our heavenly Father now welcomes us home through Jesus Christ!

CHAPTER 1: GOD IS OUR FATHER

And of his fulness have all we received, and grace for grace. For the law was given by Moses, but grace and truth came by Jesus Christ. No man hath seen God at any time; the only begotten Son, which is in the bosom of the Father, he hath declared him (John 1:16-18).

Of the fullness of Christ, we have received grace in abundance. Jesus Himself, came to reveal the grace and truth about who God is to this world. Only Jesus had seen God as He really is, at that time. In the Old Testament, a very small number of people had perceived glimpses and pieces of God, such as Moses, David and the prophets, but none of them had ever seen who He really was. The truth that Jesus came to reveal culminates in a revelation that changes everything. This revelation is a deathblow to religion in all its shapes and forms and the reality of it made the religious leadership in Jesus' day so mad that they wanted to kill Him.

This revelation, which is so radical that it changes everything, is that God is our Father. Before Jesus came to reveal the Father, the people of God had never thought that they could have a personal and intimate connection with God. This was the reason that the Father had to send His Son to reveal who He really is. Only Jesus could reveal the Father to us, because He was and still is the only one who knows the Father fully. We can learn interesting things about God through theological studies, but to know the Father as He really is, we must come to His beloved Son, Jesus Christ. Himself being God, Jesus is the perfect and true representation of who the Father is. By looking at Jesus, we can see the heart of the Father fully revealed.

Jesus Reveals the Father

… in these last days has spoken to us in His Son, whom He appointed heir of all things, through whom He also made the world. And He is the radiance of His glory and the exact representation of His nature, and upholds all things by the word of His power (Hebr. 1:2-3 NASB).

The way that God has chosen to communicate with us in the New Covenant is through His son. Everything that the Father is doing and speaking, always happens in and through Jesus Christ. Jesus radiates the Father's glory and He is a perfect expression of who the Father is. This is the reason that the only way for us to know the heart of God is through Jesus Christ. When this reality dawns on us, we can perceive the great love and generosity that is at the center of the relationship between the Father and Jesus. They are always pointing to one another. Their relationship is one of love, honor and generosity. The Father has glorified the Son, but the Son also glorified the Father by revealing His name and real face to us (John 17:1-5). Jesus revealed the Father in several ways:

- Jesus revealed the actions of the Father, since He only did what He saw the Father doing (John 5:19).
- Jesus revealed the love of the Father (1 John 4:10).
- Jesus lived by the life of the Father (John 6:57).
- Jesus' teaching came from the Father (John 14:10).
- The miracles that Jesus performed was the works of the Father (John 14:10).
- The revelation that the Holy Spirit brings to the believer, comes from Jesus, who in turn receives it from the Father (John 16:14-15).
- Jesus revealed and glorified the name of the Father (John 17:4, 6).
- Jesus revealed the Father through His redemptive work on the cross because the Father was in Him, reconciling the world to Himself through Christ (2 Cor. 5:18-19).

Jesus reveals the Father in everything He is and does. The Father always draws our attention unto the Son. This is how we got to know Jesus in the first place. Jesus said: *"No man can come to me, except the Father which hath sent me draw him: and I will raise him up at the last day"* (John 6:44). It pleases the Father when we focus our lives on Jesus and surrender to His lordship. When we surrender to Jesus Christ, He is bringing us home to the Father. As soon as we get to know Jesus Christ, He also wants to introduce us to the Father and reveal His heart to us. Jesus puts it like this:

"I praise You, Father, Lord of heaven and earth, that You have hidden these things from the wise and intelligent, and have revealed them to infants. Yes, Father, for this way was well pleasing in Your sight. All things have been handed over to Me by My Father; and no one knows the Son except the Father; nor does anyone know the Father except the Son, and anyone to whom the Son determines to reveal Him.
(Matt. 11:25-27 NASB)

This statement by Jesus reveals two very important things. First, it shows us that revelation is always given to the small ones. This is the Father's great joy and it means that we never will become qualified enough to receive revelation from Him, but instead we must become unqualified enough to receive from Him by grace. This has nothing to do with our level of education, or our social status, but it has everything to do with the posture of our hearts.

Being a small one means realizing that we need more revelation and that we are open to be shaped by our relationship with God. It's when we live in that place of real humility that revelation will come to us. Second, we learn that the Father cannot be found. We cannot reach Him by our own efforts. The Father has chosen to reveal Himself to us through Christ. Just like no one can come to Jesus Christ except by being drawn by the Father, no one can ever see the Father, except through Jesus revealing Him. Therefore, a true relationship with the Father can never be grabbed or earned.

We are invited into that relationship by grace and we receive it through faith.

We Were Chosen by the Father

Because of this, even if we made the choice of responding to the invitation to become children of God, we were enabled to do that only because the Father chose us first:

Ye have not chosen me, but I have chosen you, and ordained you, that ye should go and bring forth fruit, and that your fruit should remain: that whatsoever ye shall ask of the Father in my name, he may give it you (John 15:16).

The Father's dream has always been to have a big family. He did not become a Father because he had children. God have children because He is our Father. He was dreaming and looking forward to bringing you into His family, already before He even created the world.

Even before he made the world, God loved us and chose us in Christ to be holy and without fault in his eyes. God decided in advance to adopt us into his own family by bringing us to himself through Jesus Christ. This is what he wanted to do, and it gave him great pleasure (Eph. 1:4-5 NLT).

This is our privilege as believers. We have answered the calling of our heavenly Father and we are now part of His family. In this way, we are fulfilling the dream of the Father. It is by being His children and by abiding in His presence that we find our identity. It takes a loving Father to raise children who are secure in their identity and purpose.

Our Identity Revealed

It is very hard to know who we are in Christ, except by knowing the Father. There is a lot of good teaching available today about who we are in Christ and more and more people are finding out who they are in Him. This is wonderful news and I believe that much more revelation is coming to the body of Christ in this area. But it is hard to be established in our identity in Christ, if we lack revelation of the Father. This is because our identity in Christ is a description of who we are as children of God, and it is hard to be a secure child if we don't know the Father. Every time we read about who we are in Christ, it reveals a facet of our sonship and when we are established in the love and approval of the Father, we can begin to live out of our identity in Christ.

Only the Father can restore our identity as sons and daughters. When the Father is known and His heart is revealed there will be harmony and security among His children as well. We can see a reflection of this by looking at a human family. In a family where the parents are present to raise their children with unconditional love and approval, the kids will usually also grow up to become secure in who they are. If we're trying to live out of our identity in Christ without knowing the Father, we will eventually end up with another form of legalism. We can't reason or talk ourselves into discovering our identity in Christ. We only find it by being rooted and grounded in the love of the Father. We are then set free from all performance-based efforts, where we try to find our identity by our own reasoning and mental gymnastics. Our real identity as children of God is revealed to us as we abide in Him.

We Find Rest in Knowing Our Father

As Jesus continues to speak in Matthew 11, He lets us know what will happen to us, when we receive the revelation of God as our Father:

Come unto me, all ye that labour and are heavy laden, and I will give you rest. Take my yoke upon you, and learn of me; for I am meek and lowly in heart: and ye shall find rest unto your souls. For my yoke is easy, and my burden is light (Matt. 11:28-30).

The yoke that Jesus offers to us is an invitation to share in Jesus' relationship with His Father. This is much better than just having a personal relationship with Him. We are invited into a personal relationship with God, but only because we have been included in the fellowship between Jesus and His Father. If the burden of our relationship with God would have rested on our shoulders, it would have been a very shaky relationship. We are not always that good at stewarding our relationship with God, but because we are in Christ, our union with God rests on the faithfulness of Jesus Himself. This means that our standing with the Father is as stable and secure as that of Jesus. This is a secure foundation to build upon and through Christ, we are now living in a constant connection with the Father. We are in His presence all the time. This brings us into the rest of faith. It is no longer about us trying to create our relationship with God based on our own efforts and spiritual disciplines.

Knowing God as Father Changed My Life

My life has been radically changed and transformed by knowing God as my Father. Sometimes, when I'm about to preach or teach somewhere and the people hosting the seminar asks how I wish to be introduced, I jokingly answer: "Introduce me as Martin, a son that is deeply loved by the Father". The reason that this is so important to me is that I found true rest and freedom by knowing that I'm my Father's beloved son. He truly is well-pleased with me. Ministry, whether it is preaching, writing, or doing personal counseling, has become the expression of the Father's love that keeps pouring into my life. My journey could be described as one where I have been transformed from a legalistic and dissatisfied disciple, into becoming a deeply loved, blessed and peaceful son. Knowing God as my Father has truly changed my life. That is the reason I'm so interested in sharing the insights that I have gained with you. The gospel really is good news!

Activations

- We studied John 1:16-18 and Hebr. 1:2-3, earlier in this chapter. Spend some time reflecting on these passages together with the Holy Spirit. Ask Him to reveal more truths from these verses, about how Jesus is revealing the Father. Write down what He reveals to you.

- Go back and read the list from this chapter, in which we found out how Jesus revealed the Father. I listed a few points as examples of this there. Can you think of more examples of how Jesus revealed His Father? Do your own study on this topic. Add your own points to this list in your notes.

- We read that it is hard to find our identity in Christ if we don't know the Father. Why is that? How does our identity in Christ fit together with our sonship? Take some time to reflect on this topic. Ask the Holy Spirit to reveal more on this topic to you. Write down what He reveals to you.

- The Father lavishes His love upon you in abundance. Take 20-30 minutes in prayer, where you ask Him to shower you with His love. Then quiet yourself before Him and drink in His love.

CHAPTER 2: WELCOME HOME!

"Let not your heart be troubled; you believe in God, believe also in Me. In My Father's house are many mansions; if it were not so, I would have told you. I go to prepare a place for you. And if I go and prepare a place for you, I will come again and receive you to Myself; that where I am, there you may be also. And where I go you know, and the way you know." Thomas said to Him, "Lord, we do not know where You are going, and how can we know the way?" Jesus said to him, "I am the way, the truth, and the life. No one comes to the Father except through Me (John 14:1-6 NKJV).*

There are a few important insights to gain from this passage of scripture. To fully understand what Jesus meant when He spoke about "going to prepare a place for us", it's important to know when He made this statement. Jesus shared this teaching at the same evening that He was taken captive to be crucified and in it, He describes what was going to happen within a couple of days. Through His redemptive work on the cross, Jesus has opened the way for us back to the Father and He has prepared a place for us in His house. When Jesus was raised from the dead and ascended back to the right hand of the Father, He brought us with Him, so that we are now seated with Him at the right hand of the Father in heavenly places (Eph. 2:6). This was what Jesus spoke of when He said that He would come to bring us to where He is.

The Homecoming of the Heart

We have been brought back home to the Father and right now the Holy Spirit is pouring the love of God into our hearts, so that we can embrace this reality and experience a homecoming of the heart. This does not happen as a one-time event but is something that we're growing into more and more. We are called to find our home and roots, by abiding within His love. This revelation has revolutionized my life. Earlier in my life with God, I used to feel both restless and without roots, belonging nowhere. Now I'm at home wherever I am in the world, simply because I'm always at home with My Father. This homecoming of the heart has brought deep healing and peace to my heart. Knowing that our true home is where our Father dwells, will establish our hearts in the peace of heaven.

Jesus Brings Us Home to The Father

Jesus describes Himself as the Way back to the Father. This is a very interesting picture, because if we're traveling somewhere, it is important to know where the journey leads to. Imagine if you met me somewhere unexpected, far away from where I live. It would be strange if I told you that I am not sure where I'm going, but that it is the journey that counts. Sometimes, this is exactly how we as believers are thinking. We think like this, because we haven't fully understood where the way leads us to. The reason that we need to know Jesus as the Way is because of where He is bringing us. Jesus is bringing us back home to the Father. The longing in the heart of Jesus Christ is for us to know the Father. Because of this, a huge part of the present-day ministry of Jesus, is to bring us back home to the Father's house. As we saw in the previous chapter, the ministry of Jesus was focused on revealing and glorify the Father but never on Himself. This hasn't changed. The longing of Jesus will always be for us to know His Father.

We Are Seated with Christ

And God raised us up with Christ and seated us with him in the heavenly realms in Christ Jesus, in order that in the coming ages he might show the incomparable riches of his grace, expressed in his kindness to us in Christ Jesus (Eph. 2:6-7 NIV).

We are already seated with Christ in heavenly places right now, which means that we are at home with the Father. Jesus always abides with the Father and He has prepared a place for us there, together with Him (John 1:18). So, whether we know it or not we have already been brought home to the Father. The journey back home is about waking up to the fact that we are at home already. As I wrote earlier, all transformation and growth in the life of the believer is about becoming who we already are. It's always about realizing what we already have in Christ and learning to abide in the Father's love for us. So far, we have been talking about the fellowship between the Father and Jesus, but where is the Holy Spirit in all of this?

The Testimony of the Holy Spirit

For you have not received a spirit of slavery leading again to fear [of God's judgment], but you have received the Spirit of adoption as sons [the Spirit producing sonship] by which we [joyfully] cry, "Abba! Father!" The Spirit Himself testifies and confirms together with our spirit [assuring us] that we [believers] are children of God (Rom. 8:15-16 AMP).

The Holy Spirit is our wonderful Helper, and an important part of His ministry is to support us in our weakness (Rom. 8:26). We need a lot of help from the Holy Spirit as we are learning to be at home in the love of the Father. This is because most people have been raised in a world that has conditioned them to live with an orphan mindset. This mindset permeates both the religious and secular world. Because of this, it isn't possible for us to grasp our new identity in Christ, without revelation from the Holy Spirit.

The Love of God Has Been Poured into Our Hearts

The good news is that the Holy Spirit testifies with our spirit and that testimony confirms and assures us that we are children of

God. This inner witness establishes us deeply in the reality of our homecoming. The Holy Spirit doesn't give His witness by giving theological arguments, or even through signs and wonders. His witness is given by much better means.

Such hope [in God's promises] never disappoints us, because God's love has been abundantly poured out within our hearts through the Holy Spirit who was given to us (Rom. 5:5 AMP).

The Holy Spirit has poured the love of the Father into our hearts. Because the love of God is eternal and everlasting, it never stops flowing. The Holy Spirit is witnessing by pouring the love of the Father into our hearts, until we are filled and overflowing, with His love for us. His love becomes so one with us that our spirit responds by crying out *"Abba, Father"*. The Holy Spirit is our best advocate, the one who speaks the truth into our hearts and He uproots every lie about God that we have believed in. The Holy Spirit is our Helper and He is the one who walks beside us and strengthens us, until we are fully established in our new identity as sons and daughters of God.

Awareness and Revelation, Not Just Knowledge

Because this is basic Christianity, it is easy to think of this as such basic knowledge that all believers should know this already, but that line of thinking totally misses the point. Of course, we know that God is our Father and we know that He loves all the world. Most of us can quote John 3:16 by heart, but this isn't just about knowing theological facts. There is a lot of people who knows the Bible, but that is no guarantee that they are living in an abundant life with God. Knowledge will never transform us, but revelation does and that's what we are talking about here. To know God as Father means living in constant awareness that God is *my* Father, who loves *me at every moment of every day*. It means living with an awareness that we are His beloved children.

Knowing My Father

I remember when I came to know God as my Father. This did not happen through a single encounter. The Holy Spirit brought me on an exciting journey of revelation, where the Father's heart was unveiled more and more to me. I slowly started to realize that He loves me deeply. It took a couple of years for me to accept that I am at home in my Father's house and that I belong to His family. I grew up without knowing my earthly father. He left my mother when I was still an infant. Because my father was so absent from my life, there was a father wound in my heart and I was stuck in the identity and the ways of an orphan. This became my identity, which shaped my lifestyle for many years to come. I had decided to never become dependent on other people. I closed my heart to my loved ones. This is one of the fruits of being an orphan.

My father wound wasn't healed when I got saved. I had a lot of powerful breakthroughs when Jesus came into my life. I was set free from suicidal thoughts and all the demonic powers that had tormented me, because of my involvement in witchcraft and new age, were finally cast out by the power of Christ. I was filled with the Holy Spirit and started to flow in spiritual gifts. There was a new joy and boldness present in my life as well, but the orphan identity stuck with me through this season of my life, because it takes a Father to restore the identity of sonship.

The first time I encountered the love of the Father was during a counseling session. The man who was counseling me, shared a vision that he had received, while preparing for his session with me. In this vision, he saw how the Father lifted me up, hugged me and placed me on His lap. My Father told me how proud He was of me. I had never ever experienced my father doing that, so when my counselor shared this vision with me, it touched a deep longing in my heart and I started to cry. That was the moment when I encountered the love of the Father for the first time and this encounter started the process, where I came to know God as my Father. At that same moment, the love of God started to break the orphan identity of my life. Knowing that my heavenly Father had always wanted me in the family, even though my physical father had abandoned me, brought so much healing and freedom into my life. It's not an overstatement to say that this encounter changed everything for me. This transformed me from a servant, who didn't really know if God wanted me in His presence, into being a son that lives in my Father's presence forever.

The Servant Doesn't Stay Forever

When Jesus speaks about His place as a son in the Father's house, He reveals an important principle. *"And the servant abideth not in the house for ever: but the Son abideth ever" (John 8:35).* A servant will not have a permanent place in the house of the Father. The place and role of the servant in the house, depends on how well he performs his duties. Neither does a servant have a part in the family inheritance. The servant must live and sleep in a servant's quarter and he only gets food because of the work he performs. In other words, his relationship to the father is based on his good performance. To try to live in the Father's house as a servant, will always lead to a performance-based way of relating to God. If we perform well, we can stay and continue our duties, but if we do them poorly, we will be reprimanded or even kicked out of the house. If we are living with a servant identity, we will never find true rest in our relationship with the Father. We will then always be worried about our standing with Him. The good news is that Jesus doesn't call us His servants anymore. We are His friends. *"I no longer call you servants, because a servant does not know his master's business. Instead, I have called you friends, for everything that I learnt from my Father I have made known to you" (John 15:15 NIV).* We are Jesus' friend and the sons and daughters of God. Jesus is our big brother and we are children in the house (1 John 3:1).

The Son Stays in the Father's House Forever

The son has an eternal dwelling place in his Father's house. Jesus is speaking about Himself when He makes this statement, but it also applies to us who are His siblings. As we are growing more comfortable being at home with the Father, there are many shifts happening in how we are approaching our lives as believers. We no longer live as servants in the house, but as children. There are some very big differences between living as servants or children, especially in how we relate to God and how we steward our call and inheritance as believers. We have been made co-heirs with Christ (Rom. 8:17). This means that all the riches that heaven has to offer has already belongs to us. *"So don't ever be afraid, dearest friends! Your loving Father joyously gives you his kingdom with all its promises" (Luke 12:32 TPT)!* The son will not have to worry about his place in the family. Because the Father loves all His children, there is always room for us, in His house. This is not affected by our performance, but it is only based on the love and faithfulness of God. This is the reason why Jesus said that the son abides in the house forever (John 8:35). Nothing can ever separate us from the Father's presence (John 10:27-30). We are held in His loving arms. *"For I am persuaded, that neither death, nor life, nor angels, nor principalities, nor powers, nor things present, nor things to come, nor height, nor depth, nor any other creature, shall be able to separate us from the love of God, which is in Christ Jesus our Lord" (Rom 8:38-39).* We can stay in the Father's house forever!

It Has Pleased the Father to Give Us the Kingdom

Parents will usually do whatever they can to provide the best life possible for their children. Our Father has done and is doing the same for us, only much more generously. He is a rich and perfect father. He has even blessed us with the fulness of heavens' riches in Christ.

"Blessed be the God and Father of our Lord Jesus Christ, who hath blessed us with all spiritual blessings in heavenly places in Christ" (Eph. 1:3). This was not something that the Father did because He had to. This was something that He was very pleased to do. Our inheritance was not given to us because of our long and faithful service. We are His children, *"…and if children, then heirs; heirs of God, and joint-heirs with Christ; if so be that we suffer with him, that we may be also glorified together"* (Rom 8:17). We are not receiving our inheritance at some later point in life, way off into the future. He has given everything he have to us right now, only because we are His kids and our Father is a generous and loving Father who wants His children to have the best that He can give.

Activations

- We studied John 14:1-6 and Eph. 2:6-7, earlier in this chapter. Spend some time reflecting on these passages together with the Holy Spirit. Ask Him to reveal more truths from these passages about how you are at home in the Father's house. You have been seated at the best place at His table. Write down what He reveals to you.

- In John 14:6, we read how Jesus described Himself as:

    1. *The Way*
    2. *The Truth*
    3. *The Life*

  What does He mean by that and how does these three things show us how He is revealing the Father? Spend some time reflecting on this and invite Him to give a deeper understanding on how He reveals the Father's heart to you. Write down the insights you receive.

- We discovered that there is a huge difference between being a servant in the Father's house in comparison to being a son. Study this topic in the Bible by doing your own research. Invite the Holy Spirit to reveal more on this topic. Write down the three biggest advantages of being son that you find in your studies on this topic. Pray and declare these realities over your life.

- We saw how knowing the Father's love leads us to a deep homecoming of the heart. Take 20-30 minutes in prayer and worship. Ask the Father for your personal homecoming of your heart that establishes you deeply in His love. Then quiet yourself before Him and drink in the love of the Father.

CHAPTER 3: I WILL NOT LEAVE YOU AS ORPHANS

No, I will not abandon you as orphans—I will come to you. Soon the world will no longer see me, but you will see me. Since I live, you also will live. When I am raised to life again, you will know that I am in my Father, and you are in me, and I am in you (John 14:18-20 NLT).

Right after Jesus had told us that He was going to bring us home to the Father, He promised that we would not be left as orphans. The orphan is a person who has no parents. Because of the fall of man, the Father lost His children and consequently, man was left to live without knowing the Father and we became orphans. This was the most devastating result of the fall. When Adam ate from the tree of knowledge of good and evil, he actively chose the life of independency, and that meant breaking his relationship with God (Gen. 3:1-13). Instead of being abiding in the Father's love and finding life in fellowship with Him, the unregenerate man is now forced to trust in his own reasoning to define reality.

The Father Lost His Kids - but Found Us Again

From the Fathers' perspective, the fall meant that He was being separated from His kids. He was still present and close to us. *"He is not far from each one of us; for in Him we live and move and have our being, as also some of your own poets have said, 'For we are also His offspring"* (Acts 17:27-28 NKJV). Even if God has always been close to every human being, our perception of God had become twisted by sin. Therefore, a personal relationship with man was impossible. It is hard to imagine the pain this caused the Father, but He already had a plan, as to how to bring us back again. The history of salvation is the story of how the Father found a way to bring His kids back home again through Jesus. The Father's plan succeeded and He is right now working within our hearts to heal us from every wound of our orphan ways. This happens as our hearts are being transformed by His love. The good news is that the orphan wound doesn't stand a chance against the love of the Father. By abiding in Christ, we find true healing and restoration from every wound connected to our former orphan ways. We are free to embrace our new identity as sons and daughters of God, because we are no longer orphans. As we saw in the last chapter, we are children of God and we have both inheritance and a home in the Father's house.

The Origin of the Orphan Identity

All fatherlessness has its origin in Satan himself. He became the ultimate orphan. Satan was not created to be an orphan but freely chose the orphan path. He wanted to create his own identity and take his place of authority in the spiritual realm by becoming the new lord and ruler of creation and the heavenlies. Isaiah wrote a prophetic statement that unveils how this happened:

How art thou fallen from heaven, O Lucifer, son of the morning! how art thou cut down to the ground, which didst weaken the nations! For thou hast said in thine heart, I will ascend into heaven, I will exalt my throne above the stars of God: I will sit also upon the mount of the congregation, in the sides of the north: I will ascend above the heights of the clouds; I will be like the most High. Yet thou shalt be brought down to hell, to the sides of the pit (Isa. 14:12-15).

Isaiah is prophesying concerning the king of Babylon here, but behind the king of Babylon Satan was pulling the strings, so this prophetic declaration is ultimately directed at him. Satan's plan to create his own inheritance by rebelling and rise to prominence, didn't work out well for him. Instead of rising to the heights that he aimed for, he was brought down to the lowest place. Jesus was referring to this event, when He revealed to the disciples that He saw how Satan fell like a lightning from heaven (Luke 10:17-19).

Satan and the Orphan Heart

By studying this statement of Satan from Isaiah 14, we get a clear picture of what the orphaned lifestyle looks like. We are going to do that now, so that we can compare the orphan lifestyle which is built on a deep longing for identity and significance, to the life and inheritance that we have received as the children of God. We have received by grace the inheritance, which Satan tried to steal and grab hold of through his deceptive ways. This illustrates the big difference between legalistic religion and the New Covenant. The religious mindset tells us that we must earn favor with God, but we have already been blessed with the Father's favor and His rich inheritance in Christ. This is what Satan had in his heart:

- *"I will ascend into heaven"*
  Satan wanted to become the new ruler of the heavenlies by replacing God as the lord. He wanted to ascend there through his own strength. He had become blinded by his pride and intoxicated by his own lust for power. This led to him losing his identity as an angel and worshiper. He had become an orphan. This was his choice, but he took humanity captive into a collective state of fatherlessness. Only by knowing God as Father are we delivered from this state. By knowing Him, we will find identity and our position of authority by being seated with Christ. We no longer need to work to create our own identity. We have already been given a favored position in the heavenlies. We are our Father's beloved children. That gives us both identity and position in the heavenly realms.

- *"I will exalt my throne above the stars of God"*
  Satan planned to take authority over the hosts of heaven. The stars of God is usually a picture of the angelic hosts. He wanted to become the ruler of the angelic hosts in the heavenlies, but our Father is the true God of all the angel

armies. He is the only one who rules over them. He has created the angels to be ministering spirits and their job is to serve us who have are heirs of salvation (Hebr. 1:14). We are not ruling them, but we hold a high position in the spiritual realm where they serve us. One day, we will even judge the angels (1 Cor. 6:3).

- ***"I will sit also upon the mount of congregation"***
This is speaking of the heavenly council. Satan wanted to take a place in the heavenlies where his voice could be both heard and obeyed. Satan wanted to find a way to amplify his voice, because he knew that his voice has no real authority. After the cross, things have become worse for him. Satan has been forever silenced and everyone of his accusations has been totally nullified by the power of the cross. We are the children of God and our voice will always be heard before the throne of God. There is never a need for us to try to make our voices heard, because we have the attention of our Father all the time. *"For we have not an high priest which cannot be touched with the feeling of our infirmities; but was in all points tempted like as we are, yet without sin. Let us therefore come boldly unto the throne of grace, that we may obtain mercy, and find grace to help in time of need (Hebr. 4:15-16).*

- ***"I will ascend above the heights of the clouds"***
Satan was driven by a fallen desire for a high position in the spiritual realm. This will always be the longing of the orphan heart, because if there is no secure inheritance or standing with God, there will always be a need to create a place of safety and importance for oneself. The believer has been seated with Christ in the heavenlies and there we have a place of security and significance (Eph. 2:6). We now rule in life together with Christ (Rom. 5:17).

- *"I will be like the most High"*

  Satan wanted to make himself like God and become the lord of creation. He desired to possess the nature and life of God. His plans failed. Instead, he was thrown out of heaven down into the grave. We have been created in the image of God and we have been made partakers of His divine nature (2 Pet. 1:4). What Satan tried to get through rebelling against God, we have received by grace.

Satan's song, which is always echoing in the orphan heart is: "I will…". Because an orphan has no father, he or she is left without inheritance, home and protection, which means that the orphan needs to get all of this by himself. This is what Satan tried to do and this is the worldview that man inherited because of the fall. The orphan's heart and mindset are the root of all religion, where man tries to gain favor with a deity, so that they can find a home and an inheritance. As children of God, we don't need to create an inheritance through religious performance and neither do we need to be driven by an ambition to climb the spiritual heights. We have already received the full rights of sonship and we are already seated with Christ in the heavenly places, high above all principalities and powers (Eph.1:20-23).

The Orphan Heart

Because man lost his fellowship with the Father after falling into sin, the orphan identity has become man's identity. This results in a lifestyle that is a representation of the path that Satan chose. His plan has always been to twist the image of God within man until it reflects who he is. This the reason why he enjoys watching us living with an orphan heart, because in that way, we are then conformed into the image of Satan. He wants to distort us from being an image of Christ and remake us into an image of himself.

That will lead to a heart that has the same longings and desires as that of the devil. These are the "I wills" that drive the heart of an orphan as found in Isaiah 14:

- *I will create my own identity*
- *I will grab authority and influence*
- *I will make my voice important and make sure that I am heard*
- *I will rise and become somebody*
- *I will make myself like God*

The reason for this is simple: Since an orphan has no father, he has no inheritance or protector. Neither does he have a home or roots. This means that an orphan must fight for his own identity, inheritance and to protect himself. That will lead to a lifestyle of comparison, competition, and insecurity.

The Orphan Heart Corrupts the Gifts of God

There is another prophetic proclamation about Satan that is very similar to the one we just read in Isaiah. We find it in the book of Ezekiel and it's addressing the king of Tyre. But if we look a little bit deeper into this text, we find that Ezekiel is really addressing an angelic being, which is Satan himself. This prophetic message unveils his origin, the corruption of his character and his fall:

Moreover the word of the Lord came to me, saying, "Son of man, take up a lamentation for the king of Tyre, and say to him, 'Thus says the Lord God: "You were the seal of perfection, full of wisdom and perfect in beauty. You were in Eden, the garden of God; every precious stone was your covering: the sardius, topaz, and diamond, beryl, onyx, and jasper, sapphire, turquoise, and emerald with gold. The workmanship of your timbrels and pipes was prepared for you on the day you were created. "You were the anointed cherub who covers; I established you; You were on the holy mountain of God; You walked back and forth in the midst of fiery stones. You were perfect in your ways from the day you were created, till iniquity was found in you (Ezek. 28:11-15 NKJV).

Satan was created by God to be an anointed cherub, and he was gifted with both wisdom and beauty from God. He possessed a lot of riches and he walked on the mountain of God. This is the mountain where the heavenly councils used to meet, and Satan wanted to rule that mountain. We saw that earlier when reading the passage in Isaiah. Satan was also gifted in using instruments and music. Satan was very gifted by God, but iniquity was found within him. By keeping on reading, we find out how this iniquity entered his heart:

"By the abundance of your trading You became filled with violence within, and you sinned; therefore I cast you as a profane thing out of the mountain of God; And I destroyed you, O covering cherub, from the midst of the fiery stones. "Your heart was lifted up because of your beauty; You corrupted your wisdom for the sake of your splendor; I cast you to the ground, I laid you before kings, that they might gaze at you. "You defiled your sanctuaries by the multitude of your iniquities, by the iniquity of your trading; therefore I brought fire from your midst; it devoured you, and I turned you to ashes upon the earth in the sight of all who saw you (Ezek. 28:16-18 NKJV).

As we saw earlier in this chapter, Satan wanted to grab influence and rule in the heavenly realms. His heart was filled with greed, which corrupted all his dealings, so that he started to trade with violence. I believe this is the reason as to why Jesus got so angry when He discovered that there were people selling and buying in the temple. Jesus made a whip and drew the merchants out of the temple (John 2:14-15). After doing that *"… He said to those who sold doves, "Take these things away! Do not make My Father's house a house of merchandise!" Then His disciples remembered that it was written, "Zeal for Your house has eaten Me up." (John 2:16-17).* Jesus made it clear that in the Father's house, buying and selling with the gifts of God has no place. All of heavens blessings have been given to us by grace. We could never buy his favor by doing good works or operating in spiritual gifts. Trying to do that is part of the fallen wisdom of the devil. In the kingdom of God, the only way to gain favor and blessing is by receiving heavens' blessings in Jesus Christ. These blessings are only available to His sons and daughters.

Gifts and an Orphan Heart Equals Corruption

Satan became proud because of the beauty he possessed. This is what will happen when a person who still lives as an orphan tries to steward the gifts of God. The gifts will then be corrupt because of the wrong motivations. Pride and violence will be the result of being highly gifted by God without being established in His love. This is the reason for the competition and striving for influence that is happening in the body of Christ right now. Just like Satan corrupted the gifts of God as he chose the orphan ways, so will we corrupt the gifts of God and use them to gain influence and power when we live as orphans. The fruit of that will be pride, greed and violence. This doesn't mean that we should be afraid to receive the gifts of God. In fact, we should earnestly desire spiritual gifts (1 Cor. 14:1). Rather, this should be a call for us to be established in our real identity as His children, by receiving the love of the Father.

Religion and the Orphan Heart

The religious mindset feeds on the orphan heart. I sometimes like to define religion as the "spiritualized" version of the orphaned lifestyle. This is because all religion is built on the assumption that God is distant from us and that He is disappointed with us. When mankind buys into this false assumption, it creates a need to do things to make God happy with us, so that we can earn His blessings. Every religious system is created to accomplish that.

Jesus described this when He was addressing the teaching of the Pharisees. He said that *"…they bind heavy burdens, hard to bear, and lay them on men's shoulders; but they themselves will not move them with one of their fingers. But all their works they do to be seen by men. They make their phylacteries broad and enlarge the borders of their garments"* (Matt. 23:4-5). Trying to live by our religious rules and legalistic achievements, will sooner or later become a burden that is too heavy for any man to carry. No one can keep up with the demands of religion over time. Sooner or later, those who try will end up in a spiritual burnout. But for shorter periods of time, people can be motivated to try by guilt and the longing to be well pleasing to God. However, this will only work short term and it will always lead to rebellion and despair.

Our Father is already well pleased with us and our performance or lack thereof, will never change that. When we encounter the love of the Father, religion loses its appeal. This is the reason that the religious mindset can't stand the grace of God, because grace kills religion. The redemptive work of Christ has set us free from the slavery of working on our own spirituality and performance. We have already been sanctified, blessed and made complete in Christ (Hebr. 10:10, 14).

Counterfeit Identity and Religious Hierarchies

The works of religion could never give us a right standing before God or make Him more well-pleased with us, but it still offers the fallen mindset plenty of strategies to try. One of the ways this happen is by creating a counterfeit identity through the religious hierarchies and structures, that provide formal positions. In this way, Satan uses religion to provide a false sense of identity and security to us, based on credentials and position. Jesus continues to speak about the Pharisees:

They love the best places at feasts, the best seats in the synagogues, greetings in the marketplaces, and to be called by men, 'Rabbi, Rabbi.' But you, do not be called 'Rabbi'; for One is your Teacher, the Christ, and you are all brethren. Do not call anyone on earth your father; for One is your Father, He who is in heaven. And do not be called teachers; for One is your Teacher, the Christ (Matt. 23:6-10).

As we have already seen, the orphan heart longs for position and influence to fill the void of not having experienced the approval and love of God. This is the real reason religion always constructs hierarchies and why it values leadership positions and titles. But Jesus told us to be careful with that. We should not long for titles like Rabbi or Teacher, because Christ Himself is our teacher. He then goes on to exhort us to not call anyone on earth our father. By the context we can conclude that Jesus is not talking about our physical parents here, but spiritual leaders. There is a great need for fathers and mothers in the faith today, so it would be a huge mistake to dismiss that. But being a spiritual father is a relational authority that can only be earned by trust. It is not a title gained by having a formal position.

Everyone who is looked upon as a spiritual father in the body of Christ, should be mature enough to point people to God as their true Father. This is because only our heavenly Father can heal the wound of the orphan heart. Spiritual leaders have been called to help people find a relationship with the heavenly Father. We are a family and we are called to be brothers and sisters. We do have different functions, gifts and anointings, but these have not been given to create hierarchy or offices. They are functions through which we can serve the body of Christ. It is always important to remember that God is our true Father and that we have already been seated with Christ in heavenly places. That is the highest honor anyone could ever receive and that honor has been given to us who are children of God!

Jesus reveals to us by His example, which direction our lives will take when we are abiding in the love of the Father: *"But he who is greatest among you shall be your servant. And whoever exalts himself will be humbled, and he who humbles himself will be exalted"* (Matt. 23:11-12). This has nothing to do with our religious performance or legalism, but this is about how love expresses itself. Our hearts become Christlike, in the sense that we long to pour out our lives for others in a humble service. That is the expression of the heart that is established in Christ. Love always seeks to go lower and to serve more because that is who God is. He is the Lord of Lords and yet He is the greatest servant in the universe.

We Are No Longer Orphans

We are no longer orphans. Because of this, we can serve people from the heart. Our basic spiritual need for roots, belonging and identity is part of our inheritance in Christ. We have received it by grace. Through Christ, our Father has provided:

1. *A home for us.*
    We are seated with Christ in heavenly places (John 14:1-6, Eph. 2:6).
2. *Identity.*
    We are His beloved kids (1 John 3:1, Rom. 8:15-17).
3. *Inheritance.*
    This was done when He has given the kingdom to us and He has blessed us with all spiritual blessings in Christ Jesus (Luke 12:32, Eph. 1:3).
4. *Christlikeness.*
    We are created in His image. There is no need for us to try to become like God. We already are (1 John 4:17).

Being restored from the orphan identity doesn't mean that we're suddenly achieving our own sonship by finding our way home. This happens by a revelation through the Holy Spirit that reveals to us who we already are. We are not suddenly *becoming* children of God, but we discover that we already *are* His kids (1 John 3:1). As we abide in His love, we find healing from the orphan wound. I have already shared a little bit of my journey of coming to know God as my Father. Even if I did not have the words to express it back then in the way I do now, I can still see how the love of the Father brought healing and restoration to my heart. Through this process, I could let go of the identity of being an orphan, little by little. This is not something that happens by trying harder, or by climbing the ladder of religious performance until we finally will arrive to the glorious place of sonship. This happens as we abide in the love of the Father. As the Father pours His love into our hearts, we find healing and restoration in His presence.

Activations

- We read Isa. 14:12-15 and Ezek. 28:11-18, earlier in this chapter. Spend some time reflecting on these passages together with the Holy Spirit. Ask Him to reveal more truths from these passages about the orphan identity. Write down what He reveals to you.

- We saw how the journey from the orphan identity to sonship is a process. Where are you in this process? Are there areas where you're still struggling with the orphan identity? Spend time in reflection on this with the Holy Spirit. Write down any insights you receive.

- Go back and read the list of the *"I wills"…* of Satan, from this chapter. Then compare this list with the four things that we have received in Christ as a cure for the orphan identity. These four things are:

    1. *A home for us.*
    2. *Identity.*
    3. *Inheritance.*
    4. *Christlikeness.*

    How does these four things heal our heart us from the orphan wound? Reflect on this. Then spend some time with the Father and ask Him to establish you more in these four points.

- The Father lavishes His love upon you in abundance. Ask the Father to pour His love into the areas of your heart, where you need to be restored from the orphan wound. Take a 20-30 minute prayer walk, where you ask the Father to shower you in His love. Then drink in His love deeply.

CHAPTER 4: THE FATHER LOVES US

As soon as Jesus was baptized, he went up out of the water. At that moment heaven was opened, and he saw the Spirit of God descending like a dove and alighting on him. And a voice from heaven said, "This is my Son, whom I love; with him I am well pleased" (Matt. 3:16-17 NIV).

Jesus is the Father's beloved Son, and the Father is well pleased with Him. Because Jesus lived with a constant awareness of this, He always lived in total freedom. He constantly found security, freedom and strength through fellowshipping with His Father. The outward works, His ministry and all the signs and wonders that followed Him, were all manifestations of His life in intimacy with the Father. Jesus lived like this at every moment, every day.

As He Is, So Are We in This World

This is very relevant to us, because we are created in His image: *"Herein is our love made perfect, that we may have boldness in the day of judgment: because as he is, so are we in this world" (1 John 4:17).* Notice that John said that as Jesus is, so are we in this world. This means that just like Jesus, we are the Father's beloved children and He is well pleased with us. By learning to live as His beloved children and by being rooted and grounded in the approval that comes from Him, we enter the life of sonship that we have been created for. The Bible describes this life as the glorious freedom of the children of God. Most of the bondages and oppression that now torments the believer, springs from a confusion of identity. If a person doesn't know that they are loved by the Father, it is almost impossible to live a satisfying life with Christ. If we live with an orphan identity, we will always struggle with a void that only the love of the Father can fill. No one likes to feel empty on the inside. If people don't know the love of God, they will try to fill their inner void in some other way. The most common ways to do that is by looking for comfort in either sin or religion. Before we move on with the main point of this chapter, we will briefly look at how sin and religion operate, and why they can't give the satisfaction that they are promising us.

The False Promises of Sin

While they promise them liberty, they themselves are the servants of corruption: for of whom a man is overcome, of the same is he brought in bondage (2 Pet. 2:19).

Peter is describing false teachers in this verse. They taught a kind of liberty that gave freedom to the flesh. This freedom was meant to satisfy the believer, but that type of false freedom always leads to greater bondage. If we give in to the desire of the flesh, we will be overcome by sin and brought into bondage. Sin is so deceptive because it promises satisfaction and inner fulfillment, if we give in to the desires of the flesh. It tries to paint a picture of the Father in our mind that makes Him look like a stingy and stern old man, who wants to rob us of all the fun (Hebr. 3:13). That is of course a lie, but when a person only knows the God of religion, they will end up with the impression that God is stingy, which makes sin more attractive. The result of giving in to the power of sin will be greater bondage and we will find ourselves being emptier than before, since there is no lasting satisfaction in sin. While studying sin and how it operates, I found it interesting that sin is described as a destructive spiritual force, almost like a being with personal characteristics. (See my book, *Transformed by the Grace of God*).

A Bad Substitute for the Love of God

Sin wants to deceive us by being a substitute for the Father's love, but it can never give true satisfaction. Sin might feel good for the moment, but it will always leave us emptier so that we must keep on sinning to find satisfaction. This is how the bondages to sinful desires are developed. There is only one reason as to why people find sin attractive. John writes: *"If anyone loves the world, the love of the Father is not in him. For all that is in the world—the lust of the flesh, the lust of the eyes, and the pride of life—is not of the Father but is of the world. And the world is passing away, and the lust of it; but he who does the will of God abides forever"* (1 John 2:15-17). When sin is compared to the Father's love, it is exposed as being unattractive and powerless. A sinful lifestyle can be expressed in many ways, but the way to fall out of love with sin will always the same - encountering the love of the Father. When we abide in His love, we will love the people in this world. When John tells us not to love the world, he means the world system, not the people within it. The world is governed by the law of sin and death, but as the children of God we have something way better than that. We live by law of the spirit of life in Christ Jesus (Rom. 8:1-3). We live in the kingdom of God and His kingdom is governed by His love.

The Emptiness of Religion

We saw how sin tried to replace the Father's love. Religion wants to offer fulfilment and meaning by being a substitute to His love as well, but in a more deceptive way. Religion always tells us that we need to focus on doing good works to find a meaningful life with the Father. Ever since the fall, mankind has always had a bent toward religion. This is the corrupted wisdom that came out of the tree of knowledge of good and evil (Gen. 2:16-17, 3:1-10). Religion can provide a sense of meaning and even give us a sense of pleasure short term, because with performance-based legalism comes a satisfaction built on self-righteousness. However, in the long run, the consequence will be that we become prideful when we believe that we are doing good enough and that we will end up in condemnation when we fail. Religion can't satisfy the deep longing of our hearts. Paul describes the emptiness of religion in this passage on spiritual gifts:

If I speak with the tongues of mankind and of angels, but do not have love, I have become a noisy gong or a clanging cymbal. If I have the gift of prophecy and know all mysteries and all knowledge, and if I have all faith so as to remove mountains, but do not have love, I am nothing. And if I give away all my possessions to charity, and if I surrender my body so that I may glory, but do not have love, it does me no good.
(1 Cor. 13:1-3 NASB).

Paul is giving several examples of supernatural manifestations and the gifts of the Spirit in this passage. These are good things, which we should desire to have more of in our lives with Christ. When you look at this list, I am sure you can agree that these are all things that we need to see much more of:

- Speaking with supernatural tongues
- The gift of prophecy
- Understanding of mysteries
- Possessing knowledge concerning the kingdom of God
- Faith to move mountains
- Giving away possessions and feeding the poor
- Becoming a martyr for the gospel of Jesus Christ

These are all good things and Paul is definitely not telling us to stop operating in spiritual gifts. The point is that we can become so focused on good works that we miss the most important thing. Even operating in the gifts of the Spirit, or caring for the poor, is not what God is looking for, unless it is done as a response to His love for us. It will profit us nothing because while the people are being blessed by our ministry, we will become emptier and drier on the inside day by day. The reason for this is that ministry and spiritual gifts were never meant to satisfy our hearts, and neither were they given to us because God loves us. They were given as expressions of His love for the church and as tools for reaching the world with the gospel. The Father loves us because He loves us. His love is the only thing that can satisfy our heart in a deep and meaningful way.

Abiding in the Love of the Father

I remember how I used to read Paul's words backwards here. I realized that Paul was teaching on love and the gifts of the Spirit, but I still missed the point. The reason was that I read it from a self-centered perspective, believing that it was my duty to love God more. After all, in this text Paul speaks about operating in spiritual gifts without having love, but I didn't know how to get the love I needed. The truth is that we lack the capacity to love God and people the way we should. Love will grow in our hearts as we abide in the love of the Father. When our hearts are filled with his love and affection, we will respond by loving both God and people with the love of Christ.

And we have known and believed the love that God has for us. God is love, and he who abides in love abides in God, and God in him. Love has been perfected among us in this: that we may have boldness in the day of judgment; because as He is, so are we in this world. There is no fear in love; but perfect love casts out fear, because fear involves torment. But he who fears has not been made perfect in love. We love Him because He first loved us (1 John 4:16-19 NKJV).

We must always keep as our top priority to let Him love us. That is the only way that we can find true fulfillment and grow in love toward other people. This is the reason why ministry and service should never be the place we go to find fulfilment. That will lead to inner emptiness and a performance driven culture.

Sometimes, people ask what I consider to be the most important quality of a co-worker, or a team member. The one thing that I look after in the people I'm working with is if they are willing to cultivate a lifestyle of living loved by God. I know that when they are fully focused on abiding in His love, the other issues that they might struggle with will be dealt with as well. The Father's love makes our hearts soft and moldable, so that we become willing to learn to love and serve one another. As we are growing in love, we will be motivated to reflect Jesus by being transformed into Christlikeness.

Driven by His Love

Paul was a man of purpose and he carried a huge vision. He was a very productive man, who accomplished more than most of us could ever dream of. Yet, he was not driven by these things. He was strengthened and motivated by the love of Christ. He writes that "*…the love of Christ constraineth us; because we thus judge, that if one died for all, then were all dead: and that he died for all, that they which live should not henceforth live unto themselves, but unto him which died for them, and rose again*" (2 Cor. 5:14-15). He was driven and compelled by the love of Christ. This must be our motivation as well. My wife and I have made it a habit to regularly give the ministry back to the Father in prayer. We have told Him many times that if he blesses our ministry and work, we are grateful. If He chooses to burn it up, we would be grateful as well. The most important thing for us is to abide in the love of the Father. That doesn't mean that we want to be careless, or irresponsible with our gifts. Of course, we want to be good stewards of the talents and opportunities that God has given to us. But we want to hold our functions and tasks in the kingdom of God with open hands, realizing that the fruit that our work produces always will come from abiding in the love of God. Our focus is to know the heart of the Father and the love of Christ in deeper ways.

Two Sons and a Loving Father

As we have seen within this chapter, we can be equally as bound by sin and religion. They are both offered to us as a substitute to the love of God. If we say yes to these offers, we end up blinded to who our Father really is. Jesus once told a parable to illustrate this, even though the main point of this story is the Father's love and patience with His children. Most of us are probably familiar with this parable, which has become known as *"the parable of the lost son"* (Luke 15:11-32). This is the story of a father and his two sons. Both sons were disconnected from their father to the point that they didn't know his heart for them at all. Even though they related to their father in very different ways, both had missed out on his generosity toward them. This is how the story begins:

To illustrate the point further, Jesus told them this story: "A man had two sons. The younger son told his father, 'I want my share of your estate now before you die.' So his father agreed to divide his wealth between his sons. "A few days later this younger son packed all his belongings and moved to a distant land, and there he wasted all his money in wild living. About the time his money ran out, a great famine swept over the land, and he began to starve. He persuaded a local farmer to hire him, and the man sent him into his fields to feed the pigs. The young man became so hungry that even the pods he was feeding the pigs looked good to him. But no one gave him anything (Luke 15:11-16 NLT).

There are a few observations to be made here before we continue to read the rest of the story. We can discover a lot about the heart of the Father and the way in which he relates to us, by reflecting on how He is fathering these two sons. He is a good, patient and a very loving Father, who never gives up on us. He is also a huge believer in freedom, which is why He will never control, or force His will upon us.

The Younger Brother Asks for His Inheritance

The younger brother asked his father to give him his inheritance, while the father was still alive. This was a grave insult. By doing that, he was basically saying that he wished that his father would die, so that he could grab his inheritance and move on with life. To dishonor a father of the family like that, was a shameful act in the Jewish culture, and it was strictly forbidden according to the law of Moses. This trespass was even punishable by death (Deut. 21:18-21). This is a picture of the believer who wants to receive the benefits of sonship, without valuing his relationship with the Father. When a believer lives with that attitude, it causes pain in the heart of God. Our Father always wanted us to steward our inheritance in Christ based on a life of intimacy with Him. As we saw in the last chapter, this is one of the main signs of the orphan heart and it corrupts the gifts of Christ. Even though God might allow us to live like that for some time, while blessing and even working miracles through our lives, it's not His best will for us. Even the Father's generous blessings will ruin our inner life, if they become more important than God Himself. Living like that is always a path to bondage and brokenness.

The Father Is Not a Controlling God

Even though the father must have been very saddened and hurt by his son's request, he conceded and gave each son their part of the inheritance. This reveals something of the heart of our Father. Even if He doesn't approve of our choices and attitudes, He isn't a controlling God. He will often allow us to move on with our foolishness, but that means that He will allow us to suffer the bad consequences of our decisions as well. We have already received our inheritance as joint heirs with Christ, but we have the choice of being good or bad stewards of that inheritance. The younger son wasted his inheritance in sin. In this way, he is a picture of the believer, who is a bad steward of his inheritance by wasting it on sinful living. As I mentioned earlier, when a believer wants to enjoy all the benefit of sonship without a relationship with the Father, it will always end up with a disaster. We can only be good stewards of our inheritance in Christ by staying connected to the heart of the Father.

The Older Brother Received His Inheritance as Well

The older son never left his father's house, but he stayed at home working there while the younger son had left. Since he was the older son, he received a greater part of the inheritance and was therefore wealthier than his brother (Deut. 21:17). Whenever he liked, he could have thrown a party for his friends. After all, the property and all the animals were his. Just like his little brother, he received the inheritance, without really knowing the heart of his father. In the older brother's case, this was expressed by him working to make his father proud. He is a picture of the believer who wants to have a relationship with the Father based on good works. This describes a religious believer. The lesson we learn by reading about him, is that good works without intimacy with the Father is as big of a problem as wasting our lives in sin. We could never earn what we have already received by grace. Our Father is a very generous God. He wants us to enjoy the full benefit of our inheritance in Christ, but He wants our hearts even more. Knowing Him as our Father is the goal for our whole existence and He will always desire a deep heart connection with us.

The Parable Continues…

"When he finally came to his senses, he said to himself, 'At home even the hired servants have food enough to spare, and here I am dying of hunger! I will go home to my father and say, "Father, I have sinned against both heaven and you, and I am no longer worthy of being called your son. Please take me on as a hired servant."'

"So he returned home to his father. And while he was still a long way off, his father saw him coming. Filled with love and compassion, he ran to his son, embraced him, and kissed him. His son said to him, 'Father, I have sinned against both heaven and you, and I am no longer worthy of being called your son.' "But his father said to the servants, 'Quick! Bring the finest robe in the house and put it on him. Get a ring for his finger and sandals for his feet. And kill the calf we have been fattening. We must celebrate with a feast, for this son of mine was dead and has now returned to life. He was lost, but now he is found.' So the party began (Luke: 15:17-24 NLT).

Sometimes when people are living in sin, they will not come to their senses until they have first tasted the fruit of their lifestyle. Everyone who is enjoying a life of sin will sooner or later learn that *"the wages of sin is death"* *(Rom. 6:23).* Until this becomes clear to the person that is enjoying his sin, it is hard to reach his heart. This is the reason why it might look like God is passive when His kids are running away. He knows that some people are not ready to come back to Christ, until they have fallen all the way to the bottom. If people living in sin are not ready to repent, they are not yet open to listen to what God has to say. In fact, their hearts can become more hardened if we put pressure on them to repent before they are ready. This is the reason that we sometimes must wait for our loved ones, just like God has been very patient with us in similar situations. That doesn't mean that He is passive. He will never stop calling our hearts back to Himself when we run away. He loves His kids too much to give up on them.

The Younger Brother Comes Back Home

When he finally had enough of his foolishness, the younger son came back home. He was sure that he could never again be a son in the house after messing up so badly. So, he wanted to become one of the servants. This reveals that he didn't know his father's heart at all. He thought that he had lost his position as son in the house because of all his bad choices. In the typical family in that culture, that would certainly have been the case. By his actions, he had dishonored the family name and the community saw him as a disgrace to his family. But our Father is not like the typical earthly father. He saw things in a very different way. He saw that his son was lost and that he was a very broken man. Even though the choices that his son had made had caused the father a lot of pain, it was way more painful for him that their relationship had taken so much damage. The father just wanted his son back. This is also the way our heavenly Father feels about us. We may have behaved in a way that have caused our Father a lot of grief and pain, but His deepest longing is for us to just come back to Him.

The Restoring Love and Compassion of the Father

The father ran to hug his son and welcome him back home. He didn't start by blaming him for all the bad choices he had made. In fact, He didn't even mention them. This is how God handles us when we come to Him after we have sinned. He is full of love and compassion, and He is not interested to blame us for any of our failures. Our Father does not do shaming and condemnation, because that isn't who He is (Rom. 8:1). He is a loving Father who just wants us to come home, so that He can restore us. Our Father is the safest person in the universe to talk to if we have sinned. He is the Father of mercy and, the God of all comfort who longs to heal and restore us (2 Cor. 1:3). The younger son was not just forgiven. To be forgiven was of course of vital importance to the son and it probably brought a lot of relief and healing to him. But just being forgiven would never have restored him back into his place as a son in the house. He could have been forgiven, but still have been left in a place of brokenness and humiliation. This is probably what he expected to happen, but it would have been unacceptable to the father to allow his son to be treated like that. The father was way too merciful and generous to leave his son in a place of disgrace and brokenness. The son was welcomed back as a son again with all the rights and privileges that follows with it. This is how the Father is handling us when we come to Him, after we have failed. He forgives us and heal our hearts and then He restores us back into our full identity and inheritance as His blessed sons and daughters. Our Father is the God of Restoration and Second Chances.

The Homecoming of Lost Sons Causes Celebration

When the son came back home again, the father and his servants rejoiced greatly. They decided that they wanted to celebrate this wonderful homecoming in a big way. So, they decided to throw a party, with lots of good food, music and dancing. When a child of God, who has been wandering away into sin and brokenness returns home, there is a great celebration in heaven. This reveals how much it means to the Father to have a personal relationship with his children. The Father is not celebrating that His children has stopped sinning, but that the relationship has been restored, because one of our Father's great joys is to spend time with us.

The Parable Unfolds

"Meanwhile, the older son was in the fields working. When he returned home, he heard music and dancing in the house, and he asked one of the servants what was going on. 'Your brother is back,' he was told, 'and your father has killed the fattened calf. We are celebrating because of his safe return.' "The older brother was angry and wouldn't go in. His father came out and begged him, but he replied, 'All these years I've slaved for you and never once refused to do a single thing you told me to. And in all that time you never gave me even one young goat for a feast with my friends. Yet when this son of yours comes back after squandering your money on prostitutes, you celebrate by killing the fattened calf!' "His father said to him, 'Look, dear son, you have always stayed by me, and everything I have is yours. We had to celebrate this

happy day. For your brother was dead and has come back to life! He was lost, but now he is found (Luke 15. 25-32 NLT.)

The older son was so busy working that he missed the party. We saw earlier that this son is a picture of a believer who is stuck in legalism and religion. Legalism will cause us to miss the party by blinding us to the mercy and generosity of the Father. If we get so busy working for God that we lose connection with the heart of the Father, we will never be able to enjoy the good news of the gospel. We can be just as lost in religious programs and legalistic service, as the believer who wastes his life living in sin. The older son was just as lost and disconnected from his father's heart, as the younger one had been before he came to his senses.

Angry Because of the Father's Unconditional Love and Compassion

When we live in legalism, the unconditional love of the Father provokes anger and jealousy in our hearts. Legalism and religion are always built on the assumption that our Father is stingy and must be convinced to bless us by our good behavior. Because of this, religion pushes us into self-righteousness which in turn will make us angry with the people not working as hard as us. If they get blessed and celebrate their relationship with the Father, we're getting jealous. This explains why some people react with anger when hearing about the grace and love of God. Encountering His love kills religion and it destroys every foundation built on good works. Even the transformation and sanctification of the believer is a work of grace. The problem is that when we are disconnected from the Father's heart, we cannot experience the transforming power of His grace. The grace of God is not a doctrine but it's His active power operating on our behalf, so that we can live the life that God has called us to (Rom. 5:20-21). The way to access the power of grace goes through us learning to abide in His love and mercy, which is why the younger son finally received the father's generosity, while the older couldn't see the loving heart of their generous father.

Religion Paints a Hard and Stingy Picture of God

It seems like the older son had forgotten that he had received his inheritance as well. The father had split all his wealth and given each son their part. As the older son, he had inherited a bigger part of the wealth. The older son could have thrown a party with his friends whenever he wanted to, but he was too busy working and trying to be a good son. Once again, this illustrates perfectly how religion operates. We can miss all the blessings and benefits of the New Covenant by being busy trying to be good believers, who is doing our best to serve God. We need to remember that our hearts are always more important to God than our service.

The Father Wants All His Children at the Party

The father never gave up on bringing both his sons into the party. It was very important to him that the older son also joined in the celebration. The Father's unconditional love and mercy reaches out and welcomes angry and legalistic sons, in the same way that it welcomes the ones that have wasted their inheritance on sinful living. At times, it is challenging to deal with angry and legalistic believers, but they are just as welcome to join the celebration as the ones who have wasted their lives by living in sin. We always need to keep our hearts open to all the children of God, always hoping and praying that they will be brought home and receive a full revelation of the heart of the Father.

An Open Ending to the Story

The story ends with the father and the older son standing outside the house talking. I believe that Jesus left the ending to the story open, as a way of inviting the religious leaders that he addressed here to join the party. He shared the story of the older brother as a picture of their legalistic way of relating to the Father. The same invitation is now given to us. Jesus is inviting us to give up both sin and legalism and to join the Father's party. Neither sin, nor religion could ever fully satisfy our hearts. The only place where we find true rest and fulfillment is in the presence of the Father. I have tried both the pleasures of sin and the self-righteousness of religion, but I was left empty, broken and depressed by both. Only when I returned home to the Father, did I find the love that could satisfy my soul and give true fulfillment in my heart. There is an abundance of joy in the presence of the Father and we have been invited to join the party together with Him!

Activations

- We read from Matt. 3:16-17 and Luke 15:11-32, in this chapter. Spend some time reflecting on these passages together with the Holy Spirit. Ask Him to reveal more truths from these passages about His love for you and how well-pleased He always is with you. Write down what He reveals to you.

- We saw how operating in a powerful ministry and the gifts of the Spirit, without abiding in His love will not make us fulfilled. Only the Father's love can give true fulfillment. We noticed this by reading 1 Cor. 13. Read this chapter together with the Father a couple of times. Invite Him to speak to you through this chapter. Write down the revelation you receive from Him.

- While reading the parable of the lost son, we followed the journey of two sons. One was lost in sin, while the other was just as stuck in religion. There is actually a third son involved in this story as well. That is Jesus, who told the parable. Which one of these sons do you relate to the most?

    1. *The Lost Son.*
    2. *The Religious Son.*
    3. *Jesus-the Third Son who knows the Father's heart.*

Do you identify with one of them? Maybe two? Or do you have a little of all three within you? Spend time to reflect on this. Talk to the Father about it and ask Him to establish you more in the sonship of Jesus. Soak in His love and receive new revelations from His heart.

CHAPTER 5: OUR NEW IDENTITY

So from now on we regard no one from a human point of view [according to worldly standards and values]. Though we have known Christ from a human point of view, now we no longer know Him in this way. Therefore if anyone is in Christ [that is, grafted in, joined to Him by faith in Him as Savior], he is a new creature [reborn and renewed by the Holy Spirit]; the old things [the previous moral and spiritual condition] have passed away. Behold, new things have come [because spiritual awakening brings a new life] (2 Cor. 5:16-17 AMP).

We have already looked at the inheritance that we have received as sons and daughters. A very important part of that inheritance is our new identity in Christ. It's much harder to live as free and restored children of God, if we don't know who we are. Earlier, we saw that to know our real identity, we need to know God as our Father. However, once we know Him it is just as hard to live as sons and daughters, without a deep revelation on who we are in Christ. In my previous book, I wrote several chapters on how we now have died from our old life with Christ. I will not repeat that teaching here, but we need to know that we have died from the power and rule of sin. We have now been raised to a new life in Christ (Rom. 6:1-11). Our old man has been crucified and we have now received a totally new life in Christ, which means that we have become a new man. Because of this, we have received a new identity from the Father.

Three Sources of Identity

There are three sources of identity that we will find in the Bible. Each one of these sources provide a way of looking at people that will lead to a certain perspective on identity. Which one of these sources we listen to, will determine how we perceive ourselves, as well as how we relate to other people. While we are looking at each of these perspectives, we can probably easily recognize both perspectives that emerges from listening to the wrong voices. In fact, these perspectives are present everywhere in this world, but learning to define people God's way is more challenging. This is because our God sees things very differently, compared to how the world looks at things. Perceiving people through the eyes of the Father, means learning to look at them through their identity in Christ and their prophetic future. When writing on these three different perspectives, I'm referring to:

1.   *Satan's perspective*
2.   *The human perspective*
3.   *God's perspective*

We are now going to look at each one of them a little deeper, just to learn some valuable lessons about how identity is shaped.

1.   Satan's Perspective- Our Broken Past

Now the salvation, and the power, and the kingdom (dominion, reign) of our God, and the authority of His Christ have come; for the accuser of our [believing] brothers and sisters has been thrown down [at last], he who accuses them and keeps bringing charges [of sinful behavior] against them before our God day and night (Rev. 12:10 AMP).

Satan is an accuser and liar by nature, so his way of looking at us is through the lens of our past sins and failures. He then uses our past brokenness to put an identity on us. If his voice becomes the source through which we receive our identity, we will always be defining ourselves by past sins and failures. In other words, the identity that Satan provides will always be built on a broken and dysfunctional past. If we agree with him, we will live in bondage to the past and thereby also strengthen the bondage of old habits and behaviors. Satan's goal is to get us to agree with him, because that will make it harder for us to grow into the mature sons that

God wants us to become. I remember how I had fully bought into his perspectives and opinions about me. Breaking free from my agreement with the devil concerning my identity, was one of my longest and hardest battles ever. The belief that my past defined me was deeply ingrained into my thinking and the way I viewed myself. The good news is that there is a way to find true freedom from the lies and accusations of the devil, which is to get a deep revelation of the finished work of Jesus Christ.

All Accusations Have Become Invalid

He forgave us all our sins, having canceled the charge of our legal indebtedness, which stood against us and condemned us; he has taken it away, nailing it to the cross. And having disarmed the powers and authorities, he made a public spectacle of them, triumphing over them by the cross (Col. 2:13-15 NIV).

All our past, present, and even our future sins has been forgiven. As a result of that, the accusations of the devil is no longer valid. This is the reason that he has been fully disarmed and this is also why his perspective on us is totally false and wrong. If we have learned to identify ourselves based on our broken past, we have believed a big lie. The blood of Jesus has washed away all our sin and we have been set free from living in the past, so that we can embrace our new identity in Christ. This is the reason that John wrote that *"… they overcame him by the blood of the Lamb, and by the word of their testimony; and they loved not their lives unto the death"* *(Rev. 12:11).* We can use the word of our testimony to overcome, by speaking in agreement with the finished work of Christ. Let's encourage and strengthen one another by proclaiming that the devil is fully defeated, and that we have been set free from all his accusations. This is an extremely powerful revelation. In my own life, knowing this truth has been the major key to restoration and to find my true purpose and value in Christ.

2.   The Human Perspective- Our Present Circumstances

In the beginning of this chapter, we read that *"…from now on we regard no one from a human point of view [according to worldly standards and values]"* (2 Cor. 5:16 AMP). This verse describes the human perspective of our identity and it means defining people, based on where they are in life today. This is done by evaluating their achievements or education, work, and family situation. The sum of their life right now, becomes who we define them to be. To a high degree this also evaluates what they will become in life. This might sound a little better than Satan's perspective, but it's still a very limiting way to look at our lives. It doesn't matter how much we have achieved today; God always has so much more in store for us. Jesus told us that *"…for that which is highly esteemed among men is abomination in the sight of God"* (Luke 16:15). If we're evaluating people according to the human perspective alone, we will be much to limited in our discernment. That will make it so much harder for us to help people find their identity in Christ.

Being Limited by the Human Perspective

The prophet Samuel, almost fell into this trap when he was sent by God to the house of Jesse. God had told Samuel to anoint one of Jesse's sons as the next king of Israel (1 Sam. 16:1-13). Jesse had many sons and even a prophet, as anointed and experienced as Samuel, proved to be vulnerable to this temptation. This is what happened when the prophet met Jesse's sons:

So it was, when they came, that he looked at Eliab and said, "Surely the Lord's anointed is before Him! "But the Lord said to Samuel, "Do not look at his appearance or at his physical stature, because I have refused him. For the Lord does not see as man sees; for man looks at the outward appearance, but the Lord looks at the heart." So Jesse called Abinadab, and made him pass before Samuel. And he said, "Neither has the Lord chosen this one." Then Jesse made Shammah pass by. And he said, "Neither has the Lord chosen this one." Thus Jesse made seven of his sons pass before Samuel. And Samuel said to Jesse, "The Lord has not chosen these" (1 Sam 16:6-10 NKJV).

When he looked at Eliab, he saw a man that had the appearance of a king, but he forgot that God looks at things very differently. Our Father always looks at the heart. This incident is an excellent illustration of what it means to look at people according to the human view. God had to correct Samuel and finally he found the man that God had chosen. However, as we can clearly see here, this would have been impossible if Samuel had continued to look for a man that would have fit the human perspective:

And Samuel said to Jesse, "Are all the young men here?" Then he said, "There remains yet the youngest, and there he is, keeping the sheep. "And Samuel said to Jesse, "Send and bring him. For we will not sit down till he comes here." So he sent and brought him in. Now he was ruddy, with bright eyes, and good-looking. And the Lord said, "Arise, anoint him; for this is the one!" Then Samuel took the horn of oil and anointed him in the midst of his brothers; and the Spirit of the Lord came upon David from that day forward. So Samuel arose and went to Ramah (1 Sam. 16:11-13 NKJV).

David didn't have the appearance of a king at that time, but his heart was open to God and God could shape David until he had become the king that he was called to be. David is even referred to as a man after God's own heart (Acts 13:22). God doesn't need our good looks, competence, or charisma. He just needs our open heart. The Father never calls the qualified, but He qualifies those whom He calls.

3.   The Fathers Perspective- in Christ & Prophetic Future

And because you are sons, God has sent forth the Spirit of His Son into your hearts, crying out, "Abba, Father!" Therefore you are no longer a slave but a son, and if a son, then an heir of God through Christ (Gal. 4:6:7 NKJV).

God's perspective on us is very different. He sees us as we are in Christ and He sees who we are becoming. His perspective when looking at us, is that He can see the finished product of our lives. Remember that we have defined our growth into Christlikeness, as becoming who we already are in Him. This is the reason that the Father's perspective on us is the finished product of our lives. This is our true identity. We are His beloved sons and daughters. We are no longer slaves, but His royal heirs. Both the satanic and the human perspective of us has been nailed to the cross. We are a New Creation in Christ. This is how our heavenly Father views our lives. We would do well to agree with His perspective on our identity. His way of looking at us is true and this is the only view of our lives that really matters. The Father has an exciting future ready for us. He is inviting us to partner with Him in making that plan reality. Becoming who we already are will always take place through a process of transformation, through which God shapes our character, preparing us to handle all the responsibilities and blessings of our destiny.

Seeing the Finished Product of Our Lives

I have found it extremely encouraging that I'm no longer limited by my past. My former mistakes can no longer define who I am, since only Jesus Christ has the right to do that. He is the original picture and I am created in His image. Neither am I limited by where I am at in the present. I have been blessed in so many ways and my life is way better than it used to be, but I know that God has so much more for me. This is true for all of us. The Father is speaking about us, when He declares that those "*… whom he did foreknow, he also did predestinate to be conformed to the image of his Son, that he might be the firstborn among many brethren*" (Rom. 8:29). Our Father wants us to share in His perspective, so that we can find our identity in Christ and letting His view of us become the only one that matters.

This is one of the reasons that prophetic ministry is so important. The prophetic gift and anointing will equip us to rightly discern the potential that the Father has placed within us, as well as the plans that He has for our lives. By receiving the prophetic words from Him, our faith is stirred up, so that we can agree and move according to the plans of Christ for our lives. This is how we can partner with Him to become who we already are. Jesus gave us an example of this, by declaring to Peter: *"And I say also unto thee, that thou art Peter, and upon this rock I will build my church; and the gates of hell shall not prevail against it" (Matt 16:18).* At that time, Peter didn't look like a rock at all. He had a lot of ups and downs in his life and at one point even denying Jesus three times (Matt. 26:69-75). But Jesus didn't stop relating to Peter, according to the man he knew that Peter would one day become. In the end, Peter became a rock indeed (Gal. 2:8-9). He was one of the pillars of the church that God used to shape history.

The Disciple Whom Jesus Loved

We find a very good example of the truths that we have studied within this chapter, by looking at John the apostle. When He was speaking of himself, he was saying that *"… there was leaning on Jesus' bosom one of his disciples, whom Jesus loved" (John 13:23).* John was so gripped by the love of God that being the beloved disciple of Jesus became his identity. He speaks of himself as the disciple whom Jesus love several times within the gospel he wrote (John. 19:26, 20:2, 21:7, 21:20). The Passion translation even calls John *"the disciple that Jesus dearly loved" (John.13:23 TPT).* We have a lot to learn from John in this area. Consider some of the things that John accomplished during his life:

- He wrote one of the gospels, the letters called 1, 2 and 3 John, as well as the book of Revelation.
- He was one of the original twelve apostles and he had a very fruitful apostolic ministry.
- He was one of the founding members of the first church to ever exist, the one in Jerusalem.
- During the first century of the church, he was one of the main leaders and prophetic voices in it.
- He was trusted by Jesus Himself to take care of His own mother.
- He survived many years of imprisonment, on the Island of Patmos.

John could have defined Himself by these accomplishments and built his identity upon them, but he never did. His identity was firmly rooted in being the disciple, that was dearly loved by Jesus Christ. When we are so captivated by the love of God that both failure and success matter little to us, we can truly begin to live in the glorious freedom of being His beloved sons and daughters. The good news is that because we are already well pleasing and loved by the Father, we can enjoy life, while we are on our way to where He is bringing us. Growing in love and Christlikeness is a process, and God wants us to be satisfied in our fellowship with Him, even while we are still on our way forward.

Activations

- We studied 2 Cor. 5:14-17 and Rev. 12:10-12, earlier in this chapter. Spend some time in reflection upon these passages together with the Holy Spirit. Invite Him to provide more revelation from these passages, on your identity in Christ. Write down what He reveals to you.

- In this chapter, we looked at the calling of king David from 1 Sam. 16:1-13. Read this passage again together with the Holy Spirit. What does this passage reveal to you about what is important to God? What lessons on your identity in Christ can you find there? Invite Jesus to speak to you. Write down the insights you receive.

- We saw how the Bible describes three perspectives on identity, coming from different sources:

  1. *Satan's Perspective- Our Broken Past.*
  2. *The Human Perspective- Our Present Circumstances.*
  3. *The Father's Perspective- In Christ & Prophetic Future*

  Make three different identity statements that is based on each one of these perspectives. How does the devil look at you? What is man's perspective of you? How does God look at you? Write an identity statement on each of these perspectives.

- Take 20-30 minutes in prayer. Break the power of the identity statements that describes both the human and the satanic perspectives. Give them to the Father and destroy them. Ask the Father to establish you in your identity perspective that comes from the Father. Invite the Holy Spirit to expand your identity statement and write down what He reveals about your identity.

CHAPTER 6: ENJOYING THE PROCESS!

And we know that God causes all things to work together for good to those who love God, to those who are called according to His purpose. For those whom He foreknew, He also predestined to become conformed to the image of His Son, so that He would be the firstborn among many brothers and sisters (Rom. 8:28-29 NASB).

As we have already seen, learning how to abide in the love of the Father is a lifestyle. Knowing the Father and His love for us can't be done through a one-time encounter, or by a five-step program. This is about knowing God, which takes time. Sometimes, I have met people who have assumed that being established in His love will happen in an instant through a powerful encounter, a vision, or an experience, or maybe through deeper theological insights. Maybe that could happen, but it usually doesn't work like that at all. There are as many ways to learn to abide in His love as there are people, but this usually happens through a process. I suspect that the reason for this is that an instant transformation would be too much for us. Because God is much more interested in us than He is in His plan for us, we are being led into abiding in His love one step at the time. The Father usually works through processes. Therefore it's important that we learn to enjoy what God is doing in our lives, while we are on our way to where we are going.

God Deals with Us Through Seasons

To every thing there is a season, and a time to every purpose under the heaven: a time to be born, and a time to die; a time to plant, and a time to pluck up that which is planted; a time to kill, and a time to heal; a time to break down, and a time to build up; a time to weep, and a time to laugh; a time to mourn, and a time to dance; a time to cast away stones, and a time to gather stones together; a time to embrace, and a time to refrain from embracing; a time to get, and a time to lose; a time to keep, and a time to cast away; a time to rend, and a time to sew; a time to keep silence, and a time to speak; a time to love, and a time to hate; a time of war, and a time of peace (Ecc. 3:1-8).

We need to realize that there are many different seasons to life. This is needed to provide a good rhythm for us. It's by learning to abide in Christ through the different seasons of life that we are growing in our relationship with the Father. He has always been working with His people through processes and seasons. These includes seasons of weeping and mourning, as well as seasons of laughing, joy and dancing. A sign of us becoming more mature in Christ, is that we have learned to walk through all the different seasons of life together with God, in a stable and steadfast way.

Letting Go of the Past

Even when our lives and circumstances are changing, our Father remains the same. He has a strategy and a plan as to how we can be fruitful in every season. For this reason, we need to have our security and strength in Him alone and not in the circumstances and how our lives look like right now. One of the problems that all believers and churches will face, is that of being nostalgic and longing for seasons of the past. I have met churches and believers who spend a lot of time focusing on what once was, longing for these past moves and revivals from God. We should learn as may lessons as possible from the past. We should also steward all the insights that we have gained from history well, but it's important that we don't live there. If we want to find the plans of God for our lives right now, we must leave the past behind us. We should remember the promise that the Father has given to us: *"For I know the plans and thoughts that I have for you, says the Lord, plans for peace and well-being and not for disaster, to give you a future and a hope"* (Jer. 29:11). It doesn't matter how great or glorious the past has been. Our best days are always still ahead of us. In fact, one of the greatest enemies to God's best for us is to not be able to let go of all the good things that He has done in the past.

King Hezekiah Breaks a Monument of Past Revival

We find an example of this when king Hezekiah had to destroy the monument of what God had done in the past. The reason for this was that the people of Israel had begun to worship what God did in the past, instead of worshipping Him in the present. This made it impossible for them to move on into what He wanted to do now. This is what happened:

He removed the high places, and brake the images, and cut down the groves, and brake in pieces the brazen serpent that Moses had made: for unto those days the children of Israel did burn incense to it: and he called it Nehushtan. He trusted in the LORD God of Israel; so that after him was none like him among all the kings of Judah, nor any that were before him" (2 Kings 18:4-5).

What was so special about this brazen serpent that Moses had made? It was a monument of a past healing revival. We find the story about this move of God in the book of Numbers:

And the people spoke against God and against Moses: "Why have you brought us up out of Egypt to die in the wilderness? For there is no food and no water, and our soul loathes this worthless bread." So the Lord sent fiery serpents among the people, and they bit the people; and many of the people of Israel died. Therefore the people came to Moses, and said, "We have sinned, for we have spoken against the Lord and against you; pray to the Lord that He take away the serpents from us." So Moses prayed for the people. Then the Lord said to Moses, "Make a fiery serpent, and set it on a pole; and it shall be that everyone who is bitten, when he looks at it, shall live." So Moses made a bronze serpent, and put it on a pole; and so it was, if a serpent had bitten anyone, when he looked at the bronze serpent, he lived (Num. 21:5-9 NKJV).

The people had become discouraged and started to complain. As a result, fiery serpents entered the camp of the Israelites and they began to bite the people, resulting in the death of many. God told Moses to make this brazen serpent, so that everyone who looked at it would be healed and live. This became a big healing revival and the brazen serpent had become a monument of this move of God to the people of Israel. They had even begun to worship this serpent. Therefore, it had to be destroyed. At times, it can be very hard for the people of God to live in what Christ is doing today. The reason for that is that we're expecting it to look just like the revival of yesterday. There is an irony to this, because we ask the Father to do new things… as long as it looks just like the former renewal. We need to accept that God is doing a new thing now and this will always look different from what He did in the past.

The Past Can Be Redeemed in Christ

It is interesting to note that when Jesus speaks to Nicodemus, He is using the brazen serpent as a prophetic picture of Himself, and the power of the cross to redeem us from sins: *"And as Moses lifted up the serpent in the wilderness, even so must the Son of Man be lifted up, that whoever believes in Him should not perish but have eternal life" (John 3:14-15).* This reveals a very important principle to us. Once we have moved on from our past, to live in what God have prepared for us now, we can gain revelation and many important lessons by studying the past. It just needs to be brought through the cross to be redeemed first. When this has been done, our past will become part of the big picture of our lives, that will help us understand what the Father is doing today. It might be a bit scary to leave the past behind to step into our unknown future together with God. However, if we find security in our relationship with Christ, we can rejoice in our past victories, while we're looking forward to the even greater victories and breakthroughs that lies ahead of us.

Discerning Times and Seasons

And of the children of Issachar, which were men that had understanding of the times, to know what Israel ought to do; the heads of them were two hundred; and all their brethren were at their commandment (1 Chron. 12:32).

I have prayed a lot about learning to discern the different seasons of life, and for wisdom to walk through every season with Christ with excellence. One of the ways in which we will know that the seasons are shifting is that some things that worked for us in the past seasons, no longer brings the same life and fulfillment to us anymore. For example, the old worship songs and teachings that once used to speak to you and refresh your spiritual life, has now become ordinary and dull. This isn't necessarily a sign that there is something wrong with your heart, but it might simply be that you need a new impartation for a new season. With every season, a new revelation and sound will come from God to you.

The purpose of revelation is to bring strength and transformation into the life of the believer. Our relationship with the Father were meant to be dynamic, because life is always moving forward and our fellowship with Him deepens over time. When I enter a new season in my life with the Father, I'm usually led to new worship songs or teachings that represent what God is doing in the season that I'm in. This is how God brings His words in season to me. I have even created playlists on my smartphone, with songs from my past seasons. It has been a fascinating and funny experience to listen through these lists every now and then. It is also a great way for me to stay grateful and humble, as I remember how good and generous my Father has been to me throughout my life. But it also helps me to refresh and stir up the revelations that I have received from God through the years.

Doing Things Out of Season

And it came to pass, after the year was expired, at the time when kings go forth to battle, that David sent Joab, and his servants with him, and all Israel; and they destroyed the children of Ammon, and besieged Rabbah. But David tarried still at Jerusalem. And it came to pass in an eveningtide, that David arose from off his bed, and walked upon the roof of the king's house: and from the roof he saw a woman washing herself; and the woman was very beautiful to look upon (2 Sam. 11:1-2).

At the time when kings usually went forth to battle, David chose to stay at home. King David ended up doing what probably must be considered as the worst mistake of his life. When we are at the right place doing what we are called to do, there is protection for us. This is more important than we might realize. Many believers end up in problems because they've failed to discern what season they are in. It is not always easy to adapt when life changes and many times stepping into a new season of life with God can be a little challenging. This is because in the new season, our old ways will not work anymore. The consequences of not adapting, may not be as devastating for us as they were for David, but we will still miss a lot of the opportunities that the Father has given us. It's when believers choose to have their security in the habits that they have developed in the past that religious traditions are born. It's the same mentality that the brothers of Jesus displayed, when they tried to give Him some advice on His ministry:

His brothers therefore said to Him, "Depart from here and go into Judea, that Your disciples also may see the works that You are doing. For no one does anything in secret while he himself seeks to be known openly. If You do these things, show Yourself to the world." For even His brothers did not believe in Him. Then Jesus said to them, "My time has not yet come, but your time is always ready. The world cannot hate you, but it hates Me because I testify of it that its works are evil. You go up to this feast. I am not yet going up to this feast, for My time has not yet fully come." When He had said these things to them, He remained in Galilee (John 7:3-9 NKJV).

Even if the brothers of Jesus did not yet believe in Him, they still thought that they knew what Jesus should be doing, but they had no revelation of the times and seasons of Jesus' ministry. Neither did they understand the strategy that the Father had revealed to Jesus. This is precisely how religion operates. It creates set habits and structures to the christian life, without any understanding of the times and seasons of the Kingdom of God. Because of this, a lot of churches have built traditions and denominations, that are built on old revelations and strategies. But God is always calling us to move into new things with Him, which will always require new revelation and strategies. With every new strategy there will always come new expressions of the life of God through us. It is uncomfortable to the flesh to take new steps and change, but God will always provide a strategy to survive and thrive throughout every season of life.

Thriving in the Shifting of Seasons

So it was, after three days, that the officers went through the camp; and they commanded the people, saying, "When you see the ark of the covenant of the Lord your God, and the priests, the Levites, bearing it, then you shall set out from your place and go after it. Yet there shall be a space between you and it, about two thousand cubits by measure. Do not come near it, that you may know the way by which you must go, for you have not passed this way before." And Joshua said to the people, "Sanctify yourselves, for tomorrow the Lord will do wonders among you" (Jos. 3:2-5 NKJV).

Every new season will always require new ways of thinking and the forming of new habits that comes from revelation. Therefore, we must be willing to let new revelations from the Father shape our lives. For this reason, God spoke to Israel as they were going to cross the river Jordan, that they were to follow after the ark of the covenant. They were traveling a road they had never traveled before, and the ark of the covenant is a picture of the presence of God. This reveals that to survive through the shifting of seasons, we must abide in Christ. When we have our safety and security in our relationship with Him, we can thrive in whatever season we are in. It is good to have habits and structure to our spiritual life, but we should remember that these habits and structures are there to strengthen our relationship with the Father. In other words, the goal is for us to grow in knowing our Father, not just to keep our structures and habits. When we're walking with the presence of God, we will survive and thrive throughout every season in life.

Seasons of Pain and Struggle

If we have failed or when we are struggling in life, condemnation and accusation starts to whisper in our ears. These voices will tell us that we are the only ones who are capable to make such mess of life and that we are hopeless. This isn't true, but the devil uses this to push us into isolation where we hide our pain from others. Our pain and failures only have power over us, if we try to hide them in the dark. It is there that Satan will use them as a weapon against us, but pain loses its power over us when we admit that we are hurting. By doing that, we can give God and maybe even some trusted friends, access to our heart. Once we are open with our pains, we will find healing and freedom. This doesn't mean that everything is solved in an instant, but it is a very good start. Another important thing for us to realize, is that our situation is not unique. Pain and failures are part of our life as human beings. Everybody must face struggles and if we cannot be transparent with our struggles, we will not be able to encourage other people, by giving them hope when they're having a rough time.

Learning to Enjoy the Journey

A lot of the frustration that I have had to wrestle with early on in my life with God, came from not knowing how to enjoy my life with God in the present. I was always looking forward to the next breakthrough, or to the fulfilment of some prophetic word that I had received. By doing that, I missed much of the beauty of the process. Right after Jesus came into my life, I realized that I was called to preach the gospel all over the world. I had even received several encouraging prophetic words that confirmed this. These words resonated strongly with my heart and I had such a longing to serve God. I remember moving to Stockholm, where I went to study at a Bible school called *Jesus Heals & Restores*. These years were extremely precious to me, and I still consider them some of the best years of my life. We received a lot of very good teaching at this bible school. I was also healed and restored from much of the past pains in my life. I even met my lovely wife, Linda, there.

These were also years of restlessness and frustration, because I wanted to see the prophetic words that had been spoken over my life fulfilled. I firmly believed in, and tried to live by the principle that since Christ had paid such a very high price to save me, He deserved to get fruit back from me. I thought that this principle was built on my longing for holiness, but I was living with a very legalistic perspective at that time. As I got to know Him better, it turned out that God is not at all as focused on the result, as I had thought that He would be. The Father's focus is upon us and He enjoys walking through life together with us. This is the reason that He has called us into fellowship with Jesus (1 Cor. 1:9).

Joy and Peace in the Holy Spirit

It is good to have dreams and visions about where we are going with God. These are some of the major ways that the Holy Spirit uses to communicate with us (Acts 2:17-19). We should value the promises and prophetic words we have received from God very highly. However, we can learn to do that while being content and happy where we are, knowing that God will never fail us. I have seen many prophetic words being fulfilled, while some of them are being fulfilled right now. Some of them are yet to be fulfilled in the future.

I have learned to rest in the Father's promise, that He will finish what He started within us. He promises us *"…that he which hath begun a good work in you will perform it until the day of Jesus Christ" (Phil. 1:6)*. This confidence in the Father's ability to finish what He started within us, will keep us in peace and joy, while we are waiting for more freedom to manifest in our lives. We do well to remember that *"…the kingdom of God is not meat and drink; but righteousness, and peace, and joy in the Holy Ghost" (Rom. 14:17)*. The Father wants us to be established in the righteousness, joy, and peace of Jesus Christ. This doesn't mean that we will never have to mourn or be shaken, but amidst our challenges, we can have a foundation of joy and peace that comes by knowing that we are the righteousness of God in Christ. No matter what we are going through right now, our standing with the Father always remains the same. This is a great source of comfort and encouragement.

Fully Satisfied in Our Relationship with Christ

"Everyone who drinks of this water will be thirsty again; but whoever drinks of the water that I will give him shall never be thirsty; but the water that I will give him will become in him a fountain of water springing up to eternal life (John 4:13-14 NASB).

And Jesus said unto them, I am the bread of life: he that cometh to me shall never hunger; and he that believeth on me shall never thirst (John 6:35).

While we're waiting for the fruit of the Spirit to grow in our life, we can still be satisfied and fulfilled through our fellowship with Jesus. It's good to have a desire for the Kingdom to manifest in a greater way through us, and to live with a constant expectation for more breakthrough. But it is also important to remember that Jesus promised us that living with Him will give fulfillment and satisfaction to our hearts, while we are longing for more of His life to manifest. The water of life is the Father's love that the Holy Spirit pours into our hearts. When we drink of this water we are being transformed. His love sets us free from the frustration and restlessness, that comes from feeling that we're never arriving to where we want to be.

We are at home with the Father already and we are being rooted and grounded deeper in His love. This is what this process is all about, but there will be an overflow of love pouring out of us that will minister to people, bringing freedom and healing to them. This is what Jesus himself promised to us:

"In the last day, that great day of the feast, Jesus stood and cried, saying, If any man thirst, let him come unto me, and drink. He that believeth on me, as the scripture hath said, out of his belly shall flow rivers of living water" (John 7:37-38).

This means that we shouldn't expect to just be passive, while we are in the process of being restored. The Father's love is flowing through us to release healing and reveal Jesus to the world. This is one of the reasons that we need to learn to enjoy where we are, because otherwise we can be so focused on the future, that we miss the leading of the Holy Spirit in the present.

Activations

- We studied Rom. 8:28-29 and Ecc. 3:1-8, earlier in this chapter. Spend some time reflecting on these passages together with the Holy Spirit. Invite Him to give more revelation from these passages on the different times and seasons in your life with Christ. Write down the insights you receive.

- In this chapter, we looked at how king Hezekiah had to destroy the brazen serpent. This serpent became an idol that kept the people of God stuck in past seasons (2 Kings 18:4-5). Do you have monuments of the past like this in your life? Do you need to hand you're your past victories to God, so that you can step into the new thing that God is doing? Invite Jesus to speak to your heart. Write down what He reveals to you.

- Have you learned how to be fully satisfied in your life with Christ throughout every season? Are there some seasons in which this is harder to do? When is it easier to be fulfilled in your life with the Father? Spend some time reflecting on this together with the Holy Spirit. Ask the Father to show you how to be fulfilled in your life with Christ.

- Take 20-30 minutes in prayer. Spend some time with the Father and ask Him for the wisdom and anointing of the sons of Issachar to discern times and seasons. Use this scripture when you pray:

  From the sons of Issachar, men who understood the times, with knowledge of what Israel should do, their chiefs were two hundred; and all their kinsmen were at their command (1 Chron. 12:32 NASB).

CHAPTER 7: GROWING UP BY GROWING DOWN

At that time the disciples came to Jesus, saying, "Who then is greatest in the kingdom of heaven?" Then Jesus called a little child to Him, set him in the midst of them, and said, "Assuredly, I say to you, unless you are converted and become as little children, you will by no means enter the kingdom of heaven. Therefore whoever humbles himself as this little child is the greatest in the kingdom of heaven (Matt. 18:1-4 NKJV).

The disciples had a favorite subject that kept coming up in their conversations all the time and that was their ongoing argument over which one of them should be considered the greatest (Mark. 9:34, Luke 9:46, 22:24). Jesus responded in a way which redefined greatness in a radical way. He placed a child in front of them and said that greatness in the kingdom of God is to become childlike. He told the disciples that they needed to repent and become like little children to receive their inheritance in the Kingdom. This is a big challenge for us, since we're living in a world that is totally obsessed with greatness, and where success in many cases equals becoming rich and successful. It is the same ambition that caused the humans after the flood to build the tower of Babylon to create a name for themselves. Today, we have all kinds of help available to measure our success and influence. We have the statistics that shows us exactly how many people are listening to what we say and write. That is not a bad thing when we use it to reach people as effectively as possible. But if we think that true success in the Kingdom of God equals numbers, we are deceived, because Jesus had a very different definition of success.

We Grow up by Growing Down

In the Kingdom of God, growing up means growing down and become like a little child. This is part of the process of learning to abide in the love of the Father. His love strips us of all our false identities that we have created. He reduces us down to one thing, that we are His beloved children. This is very liberating, because we no longer need to pretend to be something that we aren't, but it is also very challenging. To be loved unconditionally, we need to let go of everything that we hold on to, in our attempts to earn the favor and approval of God. One of the things that touches my heart deeply when reading the Bible, is how the Father delights in choosing people that are totally unqualified to fulfill His plans and purposes. This touches me so deep because I know that I am one of the most unqualified people myself. If we are to be honest, we are all unqualified when it comes to living in the kingdom of God. Therefore, it is extremely encouraging to realize what kinds of people our Father loves to hang out with:

Brothers and sisters, think of what you were when you were called. Not many of you were wise by human standards; not many were influential; not many were of noble birth. But God chose the foolish things of the world to shame the wise; God chose the weak things of the world to shame the strong. God chose the lowly things of this world and the despised things—and the things that are not—to nullify the things that are, so that no one may boast before him (1 Cor. 1:26-29 NIV).

This reveals to us how radically different our Father is thinking when He builds His family. God operates in grace and humility, which is why He always chooses people by grace alone. This is a list of the characteristics and qualifications that the Father wants, when choosing the people that He wants to be on His team:

1. *He is not impressed by influencers, or people in positions of power (…not many mighty).*
2. *He also prefers that there shouldn't be to many who are wise according to the standard of this world (… not many wise according to the flesh).*
3. *And He doesn't prefer those who comes from the*

4. *He wants the foolish ones.*
5. *He wants the weak ones.*
6. *He wants the powerless ones.*
7. *He also wants the despised ones and those who count for nothing in the world.*

Most of us would make it into this list without any problem. That our Father prefers insignificant, weak, and unimpressive people reveals so much about His great humility. Usually, the powerful people want to surround themselves with influencers, the rich and the smart people of this world, but our Father feels the most at home with the lowly and simple people. These character traits have nothing to do with how much money we have, or our social status. This is all about the posture of our hearts.

The list above provides a good summary of what it looks like, to grow down and becoming childlike. When we keep on reading, Paul is revealing the big secret of how to live in childlikeness. We do that by simply giving up trying to become good christians and by allowing Jesus to express His life within us. It basically means allowing Jesus to be whatever He wants to be, in and through us.

God has united you with Christ Jesus. For our benefit God made him to be wisdom itself. Christ made us right with God; he made us pure and holy, and he freed us from sin. Therefore, as the Scriptures say, "If you want to boast, boast only about the Lord" (1 Cor. 1:30-31 NLT).

When we grow down to become small and childlike before Him, we give Christ permission to be our wisdom and sanctification. He will use that opportunity to transform us into His image and to equip us for every good work in the Kingdom of God. Jesus Christ Himself is sufficient for our every need and only someone who has taken the posture of a child, receives the full benefit of having Christ living within them. If we choose the opposite path by trusting in our wisdom and strength to live for God, Jesus will not have the space He needs within us.

Two Journeys in the Opposite Directions

Since the fall, every human being has carried a longing to become successful in the eyes of the world. This longing is the fruit of the law of sin and death. When man lost connection with the Father's heart, our need for approval and belonging was left unfulfilled. Since then, man has always been searching for significance. With success and greatness in this world comes the approval of man, which is the big reason that many people become obsessed with success and tries to create a good image and public persona. This is a temptation for all of us but the Father is leading us in the very opposite direction.

In His Kingdom, our need for identity, significance and to find a home is met when we're being rooted in the Father's love. As we abide in the love of God, we find true success which is to live as beloved and favored children of God. This sets us free from being driven by the fleshly desire for greatness and significance in this world. We find true significance by being His beloved sons and daughters, knowing that we are now favored and valued by our heavenly Father. When we live with a childlike heart, we will be invited to do great things together with Him, but we will be free from the desire for greatness and reputation, as our motivation in life. Our motivation will be to grow in intimacy with God.

How Childlike People Relate to One Another

In an earlier chapter, we read from the words of Jesus in Matthew 23. We are now going to read them again, but this time from the Passion translation:

They crave the seats of highest honor at banquets and in their meeting places. And how they love to be admired by men with their titles of respect, aspiring to be recognized in public and have others call them 'Reverend.' "But you are to be different from that. You are not to be called 'master,' for you have only one Master, and you are all brothers and sisters. And you are not to be addressed as 'father,' for you have one Father, who is in heaven. Nor are you to be addressed as 'teacher,' for you have one Teacher, the Anointed One. The greatest among you will be the one who always serves others. Remember this: If you have a lofty opinion of yourself and seek to be honored, you will be humbled. But if you have a modest opinion of yourself and choose to humble yourself, you will be honored" (Matt. 23:6-12 The Passion).

When we're reading Jesus' words to these religious leaders, by which He exposes the longing in their heart to be greeted with a formal title and to be honored as leaders, it is easy to dismiss this as something that we would never do. That would be a mistake. History has proven time and time again that religious hierarchies is a breeding ground for the culture of entitlement to grow in our hearts. The titles in themselves aren't the problem here. The point is that when we become rooted in the love of Christ, we will not place our identity in our calling, but simply view our ministry as a job description. The problem is that it's easy to forget where we have our identity, and instead trying to find our value in the titles and positions within the religious system. For this reason, Jesus shared these three important truths about how we are to relate to one another in the Kingdom of God:

1.   *We are brothers and sisters.*

This is how we are to relate to one another within the body of Christ. We need to honor, love and respect every believer since we are our Father's kids. We have different functions and we should appreciate and honor the callings of all our brothers and sisters in Christ. However, gifts and functions were never meant to provide identity for us. Our identity is always in Christ, as brothers and sisters.

2.   *God is our Father.*

Jesus gives us the advice to be careful with allowing others to address us with titles like spiritual fathers and mothers. Jesus is not saying this to claim that we shouldn't have any fathers and mothers in the body of Christ. We need mentors that can share their experience and wisdom with the people of God. I have personally been blessed to have some people in my life who are very good mentors. Receiving their input and listening to their experiences has been vital for me in so many ways, but being a mentor isn't a position of authority, or a formal title. It is a relationship where we grow in trust for a certain believer. That individual might then grow into a mentor for us, but anyone who is considered to be a father or mother in the faith, should always be mature enough to know where they find their source of approval and identity. All approval and identity should come from the Father, as we abide in His love. Everyone who is in some way looked upon as a father in the faith, must remember to point to our heavenly Father as the only true spiritual Father.

3.   *Jesus Christ is our Teacher.*

All the good teaching and revelation that we have received, ultimately come from Jesus Himself and we should always recognize Him as our true teacher. This is the main reason that Jesus told us not to allow people to address us as their teacher. This might appear strange, since the teacher is one of the ministry gifts, but Jesus is not trying to tell us to stop people from operating in their teaching gift. Jesus is simply reminding us that we shouldn't find identity or approval in the titles people give us, but simply operate in the gifts that

God has given. We need to realize that all good teaching we receive ultimately comes from Jesus Himself. When people are blessed through our ministry, it's because Christ reveals His own life and wisdom through our message.

Jesus encourages us to honor one another as brothers and sisters in Christ, knowing that God is our Father. Jesus explains how we are to live out our sonship with true honor. We do that by serving people, keeping a low and modest opinion of ourselves. If honor comes our way, that is great. If it doesn't, that is fine to. We have been given the highest honor there is. We now have the privilege of being called sons and daughters of God. Our Father loves us and is well-pleased with us. There is no higher honor than that.

Relational Authority

We have been given the authority to serve the body of Christ, but we will only be able to serve people if they're trusting us. As far as their willingness to trust us go, this is as far we can go when it comes to helping people. True authority in the kingdom of God, is always relational authority. This truth is clearly illustrated in what is commonly referred to as the greatest commandment:

Jesus said unto him, thou shalt love the Lord thy God with all thy heart, and with all thy soul, and with all thy mind. This is the first and great commandment. And the second is like unto it, thou shalt love thy neighbour as thyself. On these two commandments hang all the law and the prophets (Matt. 22:37-40).

As we abide in the Father's love, we will be growing in our love for other people as well. This is not about us trying harder to love God and people, but about staying connected to the heart of God. It is by abiding in His love, that we will find our place of spiritual authority. By loving God and loving people, we gain their trust and that is how we can minister to them in a way that truly helps.

We can have a powerful influence upon the body of Christ, if the people open their hearts to us. Trust will always be the basis for successful leadership.

Hierarchal and Administrative Authority

The mistake of the Pharisees was that they thought they could be leaders based on their titles and education. They had a hierarchal and administrative type of authority. Of course, if we are part of an organization, such as a church that is doing missions work, or other types of ministries, it requires someone to administrate and to be responsible for the work of the ministry. In such case, this type of authority should be honored and submitted to, but that's an authority given to steward a certain expression of a ministry. The church itself is not a ministry but a family and every family that is healthy, is built on a love that serves and honors. In every family there needs to be order, but the unity and health of any family is always built on the parents laying down their own lives, to serve their children.

In the kingdom of God, authority operates in a very similar way. I have sometimes talked to pastors and leaders who are worried that the people they serve are being more influenced by teaching online than by the local leadership. Because we are now living in a time where the internet and social media is always present, this will not change. I even consider this to be a big blessing, because I remember the time when I had to order tapes or CDs from other parts of the world, if I wanted to listen to certain teachings. Now I can download that same teaching in seconds. Being afraid of losing influence because we have access to good teaching online, is based on a huge misunderstanding of true authority and how it operates in the Kingdom. Just because someone is a pastor, or elder in the church, doesn't mean that they have the trust of the people. Leaders need to be less worried about what people listen to and read. Instead, we need to be more concerned serving them in love. That is the basis of all spiritual authority.

The Greatness that Man Achieves

Now there was also a dispute among them, as to which of them should be considered the greatest. And He said to them, "The kings of the Gentiles exercise lordship over them, and those who exercise authority over them are called 'benefactors.' But not so among you; on the contrary, he who is greatest among you, let him be as the younger, and he who governs as he who serves. For who is greater, he who sits at the table, or he who serves? Is it not he who sits at the table? Yet I am among you as the One who serves. (Luke 22:24-27 NKJV).

The last evening that the disciples spent with Jesus — when He gave us the Lord's supper and was taken captive to be crucified — they once again picked up their conversation concerning who was the greatest. Again, Jesus responded by teaching them about the difference of greatness in the kingdom of God, compared to how the kingdom of this world defines it. In this world, leaders are on the top of hierarchy lording it over their people. This is the world's definition of greatness. The more a person climbs in the hierarchy of society, they will also receive greater influence and visibility. That makes them more powerful. This way of thinking is not God's way, but the way of the fallen man. It is a worldwide and systematic application of the orphaned heart, which always tries to create its own inheritance, identity, and influence. If we are not rooted and grounded in our new identity in Christ, we will end up bringing that same definition of greatness into our way of thinking as believers. That means that we would be trying to operate in the kingdom of God, according to the principles of this world. That always end in disaster.

It Shall Not Be So Among You

Jesus gave a very clear instruction about this to His disciples. He simply said that this is not the way the kingdom of God operates. We find a similar conversation to the one in Luke here:

But Jesus called them unto him, and said, Ye know that the princes of the Gentiles exercise dominion over them, and they that are great exercise authority upon them. But it shall not be so among you: but whosoever will be great among you, let him be your minister; and whosoever will be chief among you, let him be your servant: even as the Son of man came not to be ministered unto, but to minister, and to give his life a ransom for many (Matt. 20:25-28).

Jesus told us that the way to greatness in the kingdom of God is not to be found in worldly success. Through that statement Jesus is addressing both the secular, as well as the religious definitions of significance and greatness. Instead, Jesus redefines greatness by telling us that greatness in the kingdom of God means losing our ambition for worldly greatness altogether. For this to happen we need to be so captivated by the love of the Father, that we lose sight of ourselves. This is how we are being transformed into the image of Christ. Laying down our lives for one another will then become the natural expression of the life and fellowship that we share with the Father.

The Blessing of Being a Small One

The question keeps coming up regarding meat that has been offered up to an idol: Should you attend meals where such meat is served, or not? We sometimes tend to think we know all we need to know to answer these kinds of questions— but sometimes our humble hearts can help us more than our proud minds. We never really know enough until we recognize that God alone knows it all (1 Cor. 8:1-3 The Message).

As we have already seen, the secrets of the kingdom of God have been hidden from the people who wants to be wise, according to the standard of this world (Matt. 11:25-26, Luke 10:21-22). When we think that we have great understanding of the things of God, we will not have a heart that is open to receive more revelation. One simple way to spot the believer who is growing in maturity, is by their willingness to admit their lack of understanding of the kingdom of God. Especially when it is expressed together with a desire to learn more. We have called to be disciples, not experts. This means that we are on a lifelong journey of exploring all the riches that we have in Christ, as well as the depths of the Father's heart. The reason why it is good to admit that we lack knowledge and understanding before God, is that our hearts will be open to receive even more revelation. A healthy child is not afraid to ask questions and by being curious and open they learn new things. This is the attitude that our Father wants us to adopt as well. When we desire more revelation, we are positioning ourselves to receive revelation from the Father. A heart of childlikeness is the secret to grow in the love of the Father. We always grow up, by growing down!

- We studied 1 Cor. 1:26-31 and Matt. 18:1-4, earlier in this chapter. Spend some time in reflection upon these passages together with the Holy Spirit. Invite Him to give deeper revelation from these passages on what it means to grow up by growing down. Write down any new insights that He reveals to you.

- In this chapter, we read about the difference between relational authority, compared to the hierarchical type of authority by using Matt. 23:1-12. Take some time to read and pray over this passage. Invite the Father to give more insight into this topic. Write down any new insight you receive.

- Take 20-30 minutes in prayer. Ask the Father to bring you through the process of growing down, so that you can start grow in the Father's love. Ask Him for grace to grow in childlikeness.

- Spend time in prayer and intercession for the body of Christ. Ask the Father to baptize us in His love and for the grace to become small and childlike again. Ask the Father to bring us through a process of growing down and become His little ones.

Part 2:

Restoration of the Whole Man

And the very God of peace sanctify you wholly; and I pray God your whole spirit and soul and body be preserved blameless unto the coming of our Lord Jesus Christ. Faithful is he that calleth you, who also will do it (1 Thess. 5:23-24).

In this part of the book, we will study how abiding in the love of the Father liberates and restores our personalities. We have been created in the image of Jesus, but because sin has damaged and marred our personalities, we now need to be healed and set free, so that we can be restored back to our authentic selves again. This process of restoration is what it means to grow in Christlikeness. In the coming chapters, we will look at how this transformation affects the different areas of our personalities.

Our spirit was recreated in the new birth (2 Cor. 5:17). Our soul is being transformed and restored when we're walking with God and allow His transforming grace to work within us (Jam. 1:21). The soul of man consists of three parts:

1. The will
2. The mind
3. The emotional life

We will look at each of these three areas and how the love of the Father transforms them. Understanding this will help us to fully embrace the lifelong process of restoration into His image. This is how we grow into becoming everything that God has called us to be. We will then look at some other areas that affects our inner life, exploring how these areas are being liberated and restored by the Father's love. Only by being rooted and grounded in His love, can we grow into the people that we are called to be. This was Paul's passion. He wrote these words in Colossians:

God [in His eternal plan] chose to make known to them how great for the Gentiles are the riches of the glory of this mystery, which is Christ in and among you, the hope and guarantee of [realizing the] glory. We proclaim Him, warning and instructing everyone in all wisdom [that is, with comprehensive insight into the word and purposes of God], so that we may present every person complete in Christ [mature, fully trained, and perfect in Him—the Anointed]. For this I labor [often to the point of exhaustion], striving with His power and energy, which so greatly works within me (Col. 1:27-29 AMP).

Paul didn't try to make the believer perfect by human means, but he guided them into understanding that they had already been perfected in Christ. Paul shows us how to live out of our identity. For that to happen, it is necessary for us to surrender our whole person to God. We must allow Him to deliver and restore every area of our lives that have been broken by sin. This includes both the damage of sins that we have committed, and sins committed against us. To see what an authentic human being looks like, we need to start by looking at Jesus. He is the only man who has ever lived without being marred and wounded by sin. Therefore, He could reveal two very important things. Firstly, in Jesus we find a perfect representation of the Father. Secondly, Jesus reveals to us what an authentic human being is meant to look like.

When writing this part of the book, my goal has been to take a solution-based approach, meaning that I am not going to analyze all the symptoms of a broken soul. Rather, I want to point to the fruit of living a lifestyle of abiding in the love of God. As we keep on receiving the love of the Father, transformation will happen in our lives. We're going to study what the fruit of living in the flow of His transforming love will look like within us. My hope is for you to be encouraged by knowing that there is restoration for you. God wants you to have a vision of a life, where the pain of the past no longer torments you. You have a bright future with the Father ahead of you.

CHAPTER 8: JESUS REVEALS WHAT TRUE HUMANITY LOOKS LIKE

For those God foreknew he also predestined to be conformed to the image of his Son, that he might be the firstborn among many brothers and sisters. (Rom. 8:29 NIV).

So it is written: "The first man Adam became a living being"; the last Adam, a life-giving spirit. The spiritual did not come first, but the natural, and after that the spiritual. The first man was of the dust of the earth; the second man is of heaven (1 Cor. 15:45-47 NIV).

Jesus is our example in every area of life, but here we will look at what a healthy personality is meant to look like by studying the life of Christ. Since Jesus was never wounded by the presence of sin, nor oppressed by demonic powers, He never needed healing or restoration. There are many things that we don't know about the internal life of Jesus, since the information that is available in the gospels is very limited. But still, we can gain some important insights by studying certain passages in the Scriptures.

The Mind of Jesus Christ

Let this mind be in you, which was also in Christ Jesus: who, being in the form of God, thought it not robbery to be equal with God: but made himself of no reputation, and took upon him the form of a servant, and was made in the likeness of men: and being found in fashion as a man, he humbled himself, and became obedient unto death, even the death of the cross (Phil. 2:5-8).

The most important thing we find, is that Jesus had a mind that was fixed on the Father. He lived in total surrender to His Father and became the Lamb of God, who gave His life to redeem us.

The mind of Christ was always filled with thoughts that reflected the will of the Father. Jesus did not live by His own reasoning or knowledge, but He only did what He saw the Father doing. His mind was totally one with the Father, which is clearly seen in one of His statements in the gospel of John:

"Then Jesus answered and said to them, 'Most assuredly, I say to you, the Son can do nothing of Himself, but what He sees the Father do; for whatever He does, the Son also does in like manner'" (John 5:19).

Because Jesus lived in constant communication with His Father, the will of the Father shaped His mind and thought patterns, so that His mind became a stronghold for God. The mind of Christ was always in line with the heart of His Father. For that reason, we can draw the conclusion that whenever the Scriptures gives an encouragement to set our mind on something, it reveals to us what the mind of Christ is focused on. He is always our standard and having our mind conformed with His, is an important part of becoming Christlike. We will gain an insight into the mind of Christ by studying passages like this one:

Finally, brothers and sisters, whatever is true, whatever is honorable, whatever is right, whatever is pure, whatever is lovely, whatever is commendable, if there is any excellence and if anything worthy of praise, think about these things (Phil. 4:8 NASB).

Whenever the Bible addresses what we should think and fill our mind with, it is always a calling for us to be conformed into the image of Christ. This is not something that we can achieve by our own strength, but it will happen through our fellowship with the Father. Jesus wasn't limited in His thinking and His mind never needed renewal. His thinking was always shaped by the love of the Father. Because we are children of God, our minds will be renewed into the mind of Christ when abide in the Father's love.

The renewal of the mind is all about learning to think according to God's perspective and to see reality through His eyes.

The Will of Jesus Christ

Jesus lived in constant surrender to His Father. Since the will of Jesus was never bound or influenced by sin, He was always free to make the right choices. Whenever I use the term good or right choices, I mean that Jesus could make choices based on the will of God. This is very different from trying to make good choices, based on religious knowledge. That is legalism. The good choices Jesus made, means that He always glorified His Father. Jesus did this by perfectly representing Him in all things. Jesus always and completely expressed the kingdom of God every day of His life. He always represented the Father perfectly.

The words that I speak to you I do not speak on My own authority; but the Father who dwells in Me does the works. Believe Me that I am in the Father and the Father in Me, or else believe Me for the sake of the works themselves (John 14:10-11).

Because of this, Jesus was free to make good choices, no matter what He faced in life. This is what a restored will is meant to look like. It means that a person can make powerful choices according to the will of God. Here are some important examples of how this looked like in the life of Jesus:

- Jesus could make good choices, even when it involved a lot of suffering to reach this goal (Phil. 2:8-11, Hebr. 5:7-9, Matt. 26:36-46).
- Jesus made good choices, even though He experienced a lot of very intense spiritual warfare (Matt. 4:1-11, Mark. 1:12-13, Luke 4:1-13).
- Jesus made good choices, because he was unaffected by wrong loyalties, both to family and friends (Mark 3:31-

35, Matt. 16:21-23).

- Jesus could make good choices, since He never became distracted by the overwhelming needs that He faced in His ministry (John 5:1-9, 19).
- Jesus made good choices because He wasn't tempted to grab worldly power or gain personal benefits (John 6:15).

Jesus was free to make choices that aligned with His Father's will because nothing could control or oppress Him. In this way, Jesus demonstrated how the will of man is supposed to work. If Adam and Eve had chosen to eat from the tree of life, instead of eating from the tree of knowledge of good and evil, man would have kept the ability to make free choices according to the life of God. As we will see in a later chapter, our will is liberated and restored through the love of the Father and by His grace working in us.

The Emotional Life of Jesus Christ

Jesus showed a deep range of emotions. In the gospels, we find many different situations where this was revealed. We find how Jesus was rejoicing, while at other times He was angry and upset. Jesus was sometimes grieving and crying, but always remained compassionate and peaceful. These are just some small glimpses into the emotional life of Jesus Christ. Since the gospels focuses on the ministry of Jesus and the early stage of His life, there isn't much information about the emotional life of Christ. But we can look at the fruit of the Spirit, to find out how Jesus expressed His emotions.

But the fruit of the Spirit is love, joy, peace, longsuffering, gentleness, goodness, faith, meekness, temperance: against such there is no law (Gal. 5:22-23).

The fruit of the Spirit describes the character of Jesus Christ and it describe what a healthy emotional life were meant to look like.

Jesus felt and expressed strong emotions at times, but they were always balanced by the fruit of the Spirit. When a person is set free and restored in their emotional life, that person will be able to feel the same range of emotions that Jesus Himself expressed. The good news is that the emotional life will then rest on a stable foundation of the fruit of the Spirit. We will live in the peace and joy of the Holy Spirit.

…for the kingdom of God is not meat and drink; but righteousness, and peace, and joy in the Holy Ghost (Rom. 14:17).

In the following chapters, we will look at how the mind, the will, as well as our emotional lives are restored by the Father's love. The journey deeper into the heart of the Father will always result in us growing in Christlikeness, so that the beauty of Christ can be revealed to the world through a restored and liberated church.

Activations

- We read 1 Thess. 5:23-24 and Rom. 8:29, earlier in this chapter. Spend some time reflecting on these passages together with the Holy Spirit. Invite Him to give more insight from these passages about the Father's plan for the restoration of man. Write down what He reveals.

- We saw how our soul consists of these three parts:

  1. *Our Mind.*
  2. *Our Will.*
  3. *Our Emotional Life.*

  In which of these three areas do you need restoration the most? Have you already been healed by His love in any of these areas? What do you want Him to do in these three areas of your soul? Take some time to pray and reflect over this together with Jesus. Write down any new insights that you receive.

- Ask the Holy Spirit to reveal to you what you will be restored back into. What will your will, emotions and mind look like when you have been fully conformed into the image of Christ. Write down this vision of the restored version of you.

- Take 20-30 minutes in prayer. Ask the Father to bring restoration to your whole personality. Ask Him to fill your whole being with His love and approval, so that you become fully transformed by His love.

CHAPTER 9: SIN, BONDAGES AND WOUNDS

Now may the God of peace Himself sanctify you entirely; and may your spirit and soul and body be kept complete, without blame at the coming of our Lord Jesus Christ. Faithful is He who calls you, and He also will do it (1 Thess. 5:23-24 NASB).

God's original plan for us has never changed. He wants to restore every area of our heart, so that we can live fulfilling and rich lives without hindrances or limitations. Our Father loves us way too much to give up on us, even if we have wandered very far from where He has planned for us to go. His goal to transform us into the image of His Christ has never changed (Rom. 8:29). This will eventually happen, but we will progress toward that goal faster, if we cooperate with Him now. If not, it will take a bit longer but when Jesus comes back, we will be fully changed into His image. The good news is that partnering with His transforming work in us makes life easier, both for us and for all the people close to us. After all, Jesus is the most wonderful person in the universe and when His life is revealed even more through us, we will become the type of person that people would like to spend time with.

Forgiveness, Freedom & Healing

We have already looked at how Jesus revealed the Father's heart and by looking at the ministry of Christ, we find out how the love of the Father manifests in this world. It is more than obvious that a huge part of His ministry is to heal and deliver those who have been oppressed:

"You know what has happened throughout the province of Judea, beginning in Galilee after the baptism that John preached — how God anointed Jesus of Nazareth with the Holy Spirit and power, and how he

went around doing good and healing all who were under the power of the devil, because God was with him" (Acts 10:37-38 NIV).

"For this purpose the Son of God was manifested, that he might destroy the works of the devil" (1 John 3:8).

Our freedom is always on the Father's agenda. Wherever there is oppression of some kind in our lives, He is actively working to find ways to heal and restore us. There are mainly three areas in our lives, where we need to be set free from oppression. They are closely connected, which means that if we are struggling in one of them, the other areas will be affected as well. In real life, it isn't possible to separate them since they overlap in our lives, but for clarity's sake, we will now look at them one at a time. These three areas are sin, bondages, and wounds.

1.   Sin

Through the finished work of Jesus Christ, total forgiveness has been provided for us. All sins — past, present, and future — have already been forgiven. *"Then God made you alive with Christ, for he forgave all our sins. He canceled the record of the charges against us and took it away by nailing it to the cross" (Col. 2:13-14 NLT).* From God's perspective, the problem of sin has already been dealt with through the cross. This doesn't mean that our sin is not harmful, or that the effect of sin no longer damages us. It is hard to have a bold and intimate relationship with the Father if we live under the accusation and condemnation that a sinful lifestyle produces. Our connection with the Father will be limited, or even blocked if we live like that. Sin ruins our inner life and sooner or later it will also damage our relationships to other people in destructive ways. The wages of sin will always be death (Rom. 6:23). But God has provided a way to genuine freedom, through repentance and forgiveness through Jesus Christ.

Some of the most powerful encounters that I have ever had with the love of the Father, has taken place while I humbled myself in His presence by confessing my sin. I have made it my habit to go for a session of prayer and counseling, at least once a year. I have found this to be a healthy thing to do, since I work so much with counseling and prayer ministry myself. In those sessions, I try to be as open and vulnerable as possible, sharing my struggles and pains, so that I can receive prayer for healing and restoration. The most powerful part of these prayer sessions has almost always been when I confessed my sins and received forgiveness. In those instances, I have been showered by the love and forgiveness of the Father. This has been my personal experience of what James is describing, when he encourages us to: *"Confess your faults one to another, and pray one for another, that ye may be healed. The effectual fervent prayer of a righteous man availeth much" (James 5:16).* This is a wonderful blessing to me, and it has helped me a lot in my life with the Father.

Confession of Sin Is Not Legalism

Sometimes believers confuse confession and repentance from sin with condemnation and legalism, but they are totally opposite to one another. When the Holy Spirit convicts us of a certain issue, He is pointing to that one area of our life and His goal is to show us a way out of that sin. The result of confessing sin and receive forgiveness from God is that we find freedom. This is a way for us to experience the healing love of our Father. He doesn't want to put us down or humiliate us, but He want to set us completely free. Condemnation is something totally different. It produces a general sense of us not being good enough and the result of being under condemnation will be a life under a big dark cloud of guilt, accusations and despair. We must understand that our heavenly Father never operates by condemning or shaming us (Rom. 8:1). People often confuses condemnation with true conviction if they have been living with the legalistic version of christianity, where almost everything has been called "sin". It's understandable why people are reacting in that way, but it is never good to throw the baby out with the bath water like that. We do not confess our sins to be exposed or punished, but to be healed and restored by the love of the Father. He is the safest person in the universe to run to with our sins and failures. His favorite thing is to bring healing and restoration to His broken children.

Forgiving Ourselves

And all things are of God, who hath reconciled us to himself by Jesus Christ, and hath given to us the ministry of reconciliation (2 Cor. 5:18).

My little children, these things write I unto you, that ye sin not. And if any man sin, we have an advocate with the Father, Jesus Christ the righteous: and he is the propitiation for our sins: and not for ours only, but also for the sins of the whole world (1 John 2:1-2).

A powerful effect of repenting of our sins is that we will learn to forgive ourselves. If we walk in unforgiveness toward ourselves, it is hard to experience the freedom and peace with God that we have in Christ. One of the keys to forgiving ourselves is to learn to see who we are from God's point of view. To see things from His perspective is the main goal of all repentance. He has already forgiven us all sins — past, present, and future — and in the eyes of the Father, our sins are already dealt with. This means that if we want to agree with God's perspective, we also need to forgive ourselves. Many people stay in bondage to the past because they are unable to forgive themselves for sins they have committed or the bad choices that they have made in life. This gives the devil a legal ground to torment them. There are few things that release the amount of freedom in our lives as when we forgive ourselves. I have, at times, made bad choices that has taken a long time for me to clean up. These choices affected not only me but the rest of my family as well. But when I forgave myself, these choices lost power to bind me from the future that God has for me. Instead, I have seen how God has made all things work together for good for me and my family. These painful situations have then become steppingstones for us, to fulfill God's plan for our lives.

Forgiving Other People

Let all bitterness, and wrath, and anger, and clamour, and evil speaking, be put away from you, with all malice: and be ye kind one to another, tenderhearted, forgiving one another, even as God for Christ's sake hath forgiven you (Eph. 4:31-32).

Learning to live in the flow of God's mercy affects how we treat other people as well. It is very hard not to love people, when we realize how much our heavenly Father loves us. This will result in us walking with God in humility by learning to love mercy.

No, O people, the Lord has told you what is good, and this is what he requires of you: to do what is right, to love mercy, and to walk humbly with your God (Micah 6:8).

Loving mercy means that we are longing to see the guilty person find forgiveness and restoration. Mercy is not the same thing as grace, even though they are often mixed up with one another. To receive mercy from God means that we are not getting what we deserve, while receiving grace means that we get what we don't deserve. We deserved to be punished for our sins, but God gave us mercy. This means that we will not be punished. Jesus took that punishment for us. We receive forgiveness and restoration instead. When we are being conformed into the image of Jesus Christ, we will have the same heart toward the people who have sinned against us.

We will long to forgive and restore such a person. When we learn to live in forgiveness, we will find true freedom, because then we are no longer bound by other people's actions. We have reached an important goal in our transformation, when we are longing to show mercy toward the person who have sinned against us. This is what Christlikeness looks like. *"Brethren, if a man be overtaken in a fault, ye which are spiritual, restore such an one in the spirit of meekness; considering thyself, lest thou also be tempted. Bear ye one another's burdens, and so fulfil the law of Christ"* (Gal. 6:1-2).

Forgiveness Is a Heart Issue

To love mercy and walk in humility with God is not just a matter of choice. Forgiveness is always a heart issue. *"So likewise shall my heavenly Father do also unto you, if ye from your hearts forgive not every one his brother their trespasses"* (Matt 18:35). Forgiveness is a fruit of abiding in the love of the Father and as we receive from His love, our hearts will be transformed. This is how we can learn to walk in forgiveness. It is true that we need to make a choice of forgiving the person who have sinned against us, but it is also true that making such a choice must come from the heart. When our hearts are filled with the love of the Father, it will result in us loving mercy and walking in forgiveness. Therefore, when we struggle to forgive, we shouldn't try hard to walk in forgiveness. We just need to keep receiving the grace of God and thank Him for the total forgiveness that He has provided for us. Over time, that will give us the strength to forgive, even if we had thought that it would have been impossible to do so.

New Covenant Forgiveness

Before the cross of Christ, receiving forgiveness from the Father was conditioned by how we forgave other people. If we forgave the person who had wounded us, we were forgiven. However, if we were unable to forgive that person, we wouldn't receive any forgiveness ourselves. In the sermon on the mount, Jesus stated: *"… if you forgive men their trespasses, your heavenly Father will also forgive you. But if you do not forgive men their trespasses, neither will your Father forgive your trespasses" (Matt. 6:14-15 see also Mark. 11:26).* Wrong applications of these words of Jesus have caused a lot of pain for many believers, especially during the counseling sessions where horrific situations sometimes have been brought up into the light. People have been told that they must forgive, if they want God to forgive them.

It's nearly impossible to forgive from the heart under this kind of pressure. If we believe that eternity hangs in the balance, we will feel forced to forgive, even if it's humanly impossible for us to do so. Jesus made this statement before the New Covenant had been established. In the New Covenant, we are not forgiving to receive forgiveness, but we do it because we have already been forgiven. As we saw earlier within this chapter, Paul told us that we need to be *"… forgiving one another, even as God for Christ's sake hath forgiven you" (Eph. 4:31-32, see also Col. 3:13-14).* When we receive a revelation of how much we have been forgiven, our hearts will be transformed so that we will be able to forgive. This is possible because we see the people who have hurt us through the Father's heart (Luke 7:47). That is how we forgive from the heart.

2.   Bondages

The Bible has a lot to say about bondages. The verses below are examples of that. Sometimes, people believe that these verses are just poetic language, but the truth is that in the realm of the spirit, these bondages are real. Bondages oppress and bind people in a way that can be very limiting and frustrating.

The cords and sorrows of death encompassed me, and the terrors of Sheol came upon me; I found distress and sorrow… O Lord, truly I am Your servant; I am Your servant, the son of Your handmaid; You have unfastened my chains (Ps. 116:3,16 AMP).

For I perceive that thou art in the gall of bitterness, and in the bond of iniquity (Acts 8:23).

These bondages need to be broken. This is done by us cultivating a lifestyle of abiding in the presence of God. We might also need someone to pray for us and break these bondages, in the name of Jesus. There are many ways, through which a person could end up in bondage. For example, by living in habitual sin, or through unhealed wounds and traumas. These bondages are one of the ways that the devil is oppressing people. This does not mean that everyone who is living in bondage is demon possessed. What it does mean is that bondage is a manifestation of the activity of the kingdom of darkness. It doesn't mean that the devil, or a demon, must be personally present. It means that our lives are limited by the damage of sin and wounds. This could happen both through sins committed by us, or sins committed against us. Another way that people end up in bondage is because of painful experiences in life, but we must know that God is not the author of bondage. Jesus came to set the captives free.

Jesus is the Bondage Breaker

"The Spirit of the Lord is upon Me (the Messiah), Because He has anointed Me to preach the good news to the poor. He has sent Me to announce release (pardon, forgiveness) to the captives, and recovery of sight to the blind, to set free those who are oppressed (downtrodden, bruised, crushed by tragedy), to proclaim the favorable year of the Lord [the day when salvation and the favor of God abound greatly]" (Luke 4:18-19 AMP).

A part of Jesus' mission was to proclaim freedom to the captives, Because Jesus is a perfect representation of the Father this reveals that there is a cry in the heart of God, to deliver us from bondages and release us from every type of captivity. As we have already seen, growing in our freedom is a big part of what it means to be conformed into the image of Christ. God's longing to deliver His people and establish His children in freedom, is revealed all the way through the Bible. As we begin to recognize how passionate God is to bring us into freedom it creates great hope in our hearts, because we know that He will never give up until He has reached His goal, which is to lead us into freedom and restoration.

Encountering the Heart of the Father

One of the major ways in which I have encountered the Father's heart, has been through being delivered from the bondages and oppression from my old life. This bondage breaking ministry of Jesus Christ is the Father's love in action. Deliverance reveals His love and compassion in a powerful way. I had a lot of struggles with fear and anxiety growing up, and I carried a lot of self-hate and rejection in my heart. Through the process of being delivered from these bondages, I got to know the love of the Father and the power of Christ in a much deeper way. That did not happen only because I found freedom, but a huge part of learning how much He loves me was by realizing that I'm so important to God that He is prepared to go to war for me. Because He loves us so much, He cannot remain passive when it comes to liberating us.

We should always remember that our freedom is His passion, and that He is always motivated by His love and affection for us. Sometimes, we do not associate deliverance with the love of the Father. This is because often when people talk about the love of the Father, they do that only in nurturing and comforting terms, which certainly is a very important part of how God is fathering us. But His power to deliver us from bondage and captivity, is a powerful expression of His love as well. The love of the Father is like a burning fire. He can't stay passive and indifferent when it comes to our freedom. He loves us too much to do that.

Bondages and Demonic Activity

Even though we have seen that having a bondage is not the same thing as having demons within us, this could still be the case. We need to understand how the kingdom of darkness works. Since a believer belongs to God, demons have no right to just enter our lives to torment us whenever they want. The truth is that demons are very limited in their capacity to operate against us. They have been limited to only work in darkness. Jude describes this reality with these words: *"And angels who did not keep their own domain but abandoned their proper dwelling place, these He has kept in eternal restraints under darkness for the judgment of the great day"* (Jude 6 NASB).

When speaking about the fallen angels and demons, Jude reveals that they are bound by the eternal restraints under darkness. This means that demons can only operate in darkness. Since we now have been delivered from the realm of darkness to the Kingdom of God, we have been given the privilege to walk in the light. The devil can only enter our lives, if we allow some parts of our lives to remain in darkness. This is the reason that Paul warned us: *"Be ye angry, and sin not: let not the sun go down upon your wrath: neither give place to the devil"* (Eph. 4:26-27). The devil only has access to us if we allow him to have it, which is why he is working so hard to convince us to keep certain areas of our lives hidden. It is only in the dark that he can operate. This is the reason that confession of sins is so powerful. It is one of the major ways through which we walk in the light, and thereby deny the devil further access to our lives. He has no power over us when we are walking in the light. I mentioned earlier how I go for a counseling session once a year. This is another reason for me doing that. It is a good way to keep all the areas in which I struggle with sins and temptation in the light. Doing so keeps the door shut to demonic activity and bondages. A huge benefit of this, is that it keeps me transparent and helps me to remain humble before the Father.

<h2 style="text-align:center">Manifestations of Bondages</h2>

It is easy to discern bondage in our lives. If there are certain areas, in which we are being controlled or limited in our ability to make powerful choices, there are usually some kind of bondages there. *"They promise freedom, but they themselves are slaves of sin and corruption. For you are a slave to whatever controls you"* (2 Pet. 2:19). Sometimes we can get so used to being limited in certain areas of our lives, that we don't realize that we have a problem. A person who is deceived doesn't know that they have been fooled. Many people have been deceived to believe lies about themselves that are very limiting.

When I counsel people who has been deceived in this way, they sometimes describe themselves as fearful and afraid, or as being bound in some other way. They then proceed to tell me that this is just the way they are. My answer to that statement will often be this question: "Is this really just who you are, or have you been fooled into thinking that this is you"? Bondages always controls the person who carries it, but it is even more harmful when being bound has become such a part of our lives, that we consider it to be part of our identity. The good news is that there is freedom in Christ for all of us. Jesus has broken every bondage and chain in our lives. When the bondages and chains that have tormented us finally have been exposed, it's not that difficult to break free. We have been authority over every bondage and all demonic powers in the name of Jesus.

<h2 style="text-align:center">Authority to Break Free</h2>

Because we have the name of Jesus, we have received authority to bind and loose. Jesus said: *"Verily I say unto you, Whatsoever ye shall bind on earth shall be bound in heaven: and whatsoever ye shall loose on earth shall be loosed in heaven"* (Matt. 18:18). We can break free from all bondages in the name of Jesus. In His name, we have now received authority over the demonic realm (Mark. 16:15-20). Jesus was given the name above all names, through His finished work on the cross.

"Therefore God also has highly exalted Him and given Him the name which is above every name, that at the name of Jesus every knee should bow, of those in heaven, and of those on earth, and of those under the earth, and that every tongue should confess that Jesus Christ is Lord, to the glory of God the Father" (Phil. 2:9-11 NKJV).

In the name of Jesus, we can now break every bondage that have held us back. We can break free from all demonic resistance that tries to hold us bound. Since there is a tendency among believers to be afraid when talking about demonic activity and deliverance ministry, it's important for us to remember that this is nothing to fear. The truth is that the demonic realm is afraid of us and they are nervous about us discovering our authority in Jesus' name. They know that when that happens, their time is over. So, if we discover a bondage in our lives, we can then break it in the name of Jesus. We can also ask a friend, or a counselor to pray with us and break these bondages together with us. In my previous book, I wrote a whole chapter on our authority over the demonic realm, so I will not do a deeper study on this subject here.

3.   Wounds

No one goes through life, without being wounded in some way. These wounds need to be healed. If they are not healed, they will become infected and bitter roots will develop (Hebr. 12:15). The good news for us is that Jesus has provided complete healing for us through His work on the cross. *"Our instant healing flowed from his wounding. You were like sheep that continually wandered away, but now you have returned to the true Shepherd of your lives—the kind Guardian who lovingly watches over your souls" (1 Pet. 2:24-25 TPT).* By coming to Him we will find healing. The Father has such a heart of compassion toward all lost and wounded people. This is the reason that the great commission is important to Him. Jesus wants everybody to receive His loving compassion, so that they can be healed and restored.

But when he saw the multitudes, he was moved with compassion on them, because they fainted, and were scattered abroad, as sheep having no shepherd. Then saith he unto his disciples, the harvest truly is plenteous, but the labourers are few; Pray ye therefore the Lord of the harvest, that he will send forth labourers into his harvest (Matt. 9:36-38).

Jesus was moved with compassion when he saw the multitudes, scattered without a shepherd and He was deeply touched when He saw their great need. He saw that there was no one to provide true healing for the wounds and brokenness of the people. Jesus is the same yesterday, today, and forever. This means that He is still moved with great compassion for us today. He longs to bring freedom to those in bondage and to restore every broken heart. Jesus doesn't despise our weakness, failures, and brokenness. He longs to shower us with compassion, because He loves mercy. Jesus will take every opportunity He gets to minister to us. This is the reason that He is called the Shepherd and Overseer of our souls. When He sees our need, He is moved with compassion for us, but He will never control us. He will patiently wait for us to open our hearts to His healing love.

Healing Is Our Inheritance

Jesus was so moved with compassion that when He went to the cross, He bore our sicknesses and wounds to provide healing for us. Jesus took all our suffering upon Himself to fully restore us. These verses from the book of Isaiah, reveals to us how healing is included in the atonement. Jesus provided our full healing and restoration through the cross.

Surely He has borne our griefs And carried our sorrows; Yet we esteemed Him stricken, Smitten by God, and afflicted. But He was wounded for our transgressions, He was bruised for our iniquities, The chastisement for our peace was upon Him, And by His stripes we are healed. All we like sheep have gone astray; We have turned, every one, to his own way; And the Lord has laid on Him the iniquity of us all. (Isa. 53:4-6 NKJV).

Jesus Christ became sin for us when He carried our iniquities and transgressions and nailed them to the cross. He took our sins to make us the righteousness of God in Him (2 Cor. 5:21). He even carried our griefs and sorrows and became wounded, to provide healing for us. Every tear that we have cried, all the pain that we have ever suffered and all the wounds that has ever tormented our hearts, Jesus took upon Himself when He went to the cross. Healing is not only a judicial matter to Him. Jesus has personally felt all the pain of our failures and the weight of our bondages. Jesus has cried our tears. He does not just watch from a distance when we go through trials and pain. Jesus walks with us through our pain and brokenness. We can come to Jesus to be comforted and to receive healing and restoration. The door of his heart has always been open for us!

Coming to Jesus to Receive Healing

There are two beautiful passages in the book of Hebrews that has been extremely important to me, when it comes being healed and restored:

Therefore, it was necessary for him to be made in every respect like us, his brothers and sisters, so that he could be our merciful and faithful High Priest before God. Then he could offer a sacrifice that would take away the sins of the people. Since he himself has gone through suffering and testing, he is able to help us when we are being tested (Hebr. 2:17-18 NLT).

This High Priest of ours understands our weaknesses, for he faced all of the same testings we do, yet he did not sin. So let us come boldly to the throne of our gracious God. There we will receive his mercy, and we will find grace to help us when we need it most (Hebr. 4:15-16 NLT).

I wrote earlier in this chapter, how the Father is the safest person in the universe to run to if we have sinned. He is the best person to run to when we struggle with pain, temptation, and weakness as well. There are important characteristics of Jesus, that stands out to me when I'm reading these Scriptures:

- Jesus is a merciful High Priest.
- Jesus is a faithful High Priest.
- Jesus has gone through suffering and testing. Therefore, He can relate to our struggles and brokenness. He longs to help us.
- Jesus understands our weaknesses.
- Jesus provides grace, mercy and help when we are in need.

To know these characteristics has made it so much easier to come to Jesus with my wounds, knowing that He will be merciful and faithful to me. I know that I need a lot of mercy and grace all the time and Jesus has always been faithful to me. When I have come to Him with my deepest pains, He listens and can fully relate to me. That has been a deeply healing experience for me. We can at times get the impression that our healing is a complicated thing. But usually inner healing happens just by talking to our heavenly Father about our mistakes, allowing him to comfort and minister healing to our hearts. The gospel is always very simple, which is a very good thing, because our lives are sometimes complicated enough to deal with.

Activations

- We studied Acts 10:37-38 and 1 John 3:8, earlier in this chapter. Spend some time reflecting on these passages together with the Holy Spirit. Invite Him to give more insight from these passages about the deliverance and healing ministry of Jesus Christ. Write down what He reveals to you.

- In this chapter, we looked at three main areas in which our souls can be wounded: *sin, bondages and wounds.* Take 20-30 minutes in prayer for each area. Use these instructions as guidelines for your prayer:

  1. *Sin:* Jesus has delivered you from sin through the cross. All your sins- past, present and future-have now been completely forgiven. Ask the Father to establish your heart deep in this truth. Invite Him to deliver you from all condemnation and guilt. Ask Him to give you a heart that loves mercy and to transform you into a person, who loves to both forgive and restore the ones who have sinned and failed.

  2. *Bondages:* Jesus has broken every bondage on the cross. Ask the Holy Spirit to reveal if there are still bondages or any other oppression in your life that needs to be broken. If He reveals areas where you need more freedom, let Him lead you in prayer to break these bondages. He wants to set you free!

  3. *Wounds:* Through the wounds of Christ, you have been made whole. Ask the Father to reveal all the wounds that are still hidden within in your heart and that needs to be healed. If He reveals an area within your heart that is still wounded, ask Him

to pour out His healing love into that area. Soak
in His healing love and receive restoration.

- Spend some time in prayer for the body of Christ. Ask
  the Father to give grace, revelation and wisdom to us,
  so that we can minister to broken people, much more
  effectively. Ask Him to fill us with more anointing to
  heal the broken hearted and set the captives free.

CHAPTER 10: THE RENEWAL OF THE MIND

The Word of God has a lot to say about the renewal of our mind. Paul gives us the following encouragement on this subject: *"And be not conformed to this world: but be ye transformed by the renewing of your mind, that ye may prove what is that good, and acceptable, and perfect, will of God" (Rom. 12:2).* Our minds need renewal because we live in a world that abide by a very different set of values and mindset, compared to that of the kingdom of God. Unlike Jesus, we have not spent a lifetime of intimate connection to the Father, which means that our thinking hasn't been shaped by the love of God to the same degree.

Instead, we have been conditioned to think contrary to the Word of God. As a result, there are strongholds in our minds that need to be broken. We renew our minds by being rooted in the gospel of Jesus Christ and by abiding in the love of the Father. The goal of renewing the mind is to think in line with the heart of Father, and to see reality through His eyes. Renewing the mind does not happen overnight and neither will it be a painless process. For a time, it might even feel like there is a war between the Kingdom of God and the values of our old way of thinking. In fact, this war is very real and our mind is the battleground where this battle is fought. When the love of the Father confronts our fallen thinking, conflict is inevitable. This is the reason that Paul is describing our minds as a battlefield:

For though we walk in the flesh, we do not war according to the flesh. For the weapons of our warfare are not carnal but mighty in God for pulling down strongholds, casting down arguments and every high thing that exalts itself against the knowledge of God, bringing every thought into captivity to the obedience of Christ, and being ready to punish all disobedience when your obedience is fulfilled (2 Cor. 10:3-5 NKJV).

The weapons of our warfare are the promises that God has given to us. These promises are powerful enough to deliver our minds from the strongholds of the world, so that we can live in the mind of Christ. Our part is to surrender our minds to the reign of God, which gives us authority to bring every thought into submission to the obedience of Christ. As we surrender our thought patterns to Christ, His grace empowers us to break free from destructive thinking and to connect with our Father's points of view.

Submitting Our Minds to the Rule of Christ

We submit our minds to the lordship of Christ the same way that Jesus submitted to the Father, which is to live in total dependence of Him. As we keep receiving from His love, we will start to see the world through His eyes and all the strongholds in our minds will start to crumble and break down. The Word of God provides the information needed for the transformation of our minds, but it is when the Holy Spirit illuminates the eyes of our hearts, that the truth of the Word becomes revelation to us. This is important to remember, because otherwise we might think that the renewal of the mind is up to us. Revelation comes easy to the heart that is rooted and grounded in the love of Christ.

We must understand that whatever the Father asks of us, He has already provided for us in Christ. Because Jesus indwells us, we now have access to the mind of Christ, and by staying connected to Him our minds are renewed. There are certain areas where the way we think becomes very important. These are key areas to the renewal of our mind, which is the reason that these areas are the center of the battle in our minds. Some of these are so important, that we are going to look at them a little more specifically now:

- *God*

  Our view of God has a huge influence on our thinking in all other areas of life. If, for example, we believe that God seldom wants to speak to us and that He is hard to reach, we will not expect Him to speak to us that often. Because of this, we will not listen for His voice. If we believe Him to be harsh and legalistic, that is how we will treat people as well. If we have a living revelation our loving Father, whose heart is full of love and mercy, that will manifest in how we live our lives. As we're learning to receive the Father's love, our mind will gradually be renewed, until we're living with a revelation of His goodness and love. That will bring us into a life of freedom.

- *Identity*

  Another big area that will limit us in a big way, is when we are confused about our identity in Christ. If we're still believing that we're just sinners saved by grace, it's hard to live a life of freedom and boldness. We will then end up bound by shame and the feelings that we're not good enough for God. This shame-based identity is sometimes confused with humility, but it is a false humility. It might appear impressive to the religious mind but this is pride. It's a very self-centered thinking that underestimates the effects of the redemptive work of Christ. Living like that prevents us from accessing the benefits that belong to us in the New Covenant. There is such a power in knowing that we now are the righteousness of God in Jesus Christ and that the Father loves us. It delivers us from the false identities that we have embraced, just to survive the pain and brokenness of this world.

- *Personal Capacity*

  Another area where strongholds need to be broken is our view of our potential in Christ, as well as the talents and gifts God has placed within us. A lot of people have been trained to think in a way, by which they put themselves down. As a result of that, they live way below what God had intended for them. This happens if we believe the lie that we are failures that will never succeed in doing new things. This will then become a stronghold in our minds. Strongholds such as this one needs to be broken for us to live the way that the Father has called us to live. As we're allowing the love of the Father to minister to our hearts and listen to what the Holy Spirit is speaking, we start to live in the prophetic potential that God has placed in our hearts. We can do all things through Christ!

- *Religious thinking*
  A lot of strongholds are rooted and find their strength in our religious and legalistic belief systems. For example, if a woman is called to preach, or to be a leader, but has been hearing her whole life that women can't preach or lead, it might hinder her from responding to the call that God has put within her. Or, if someone who is struggling with sickness believes that sickness sometimes is the will of God, then that mindset will become a huge hindrance for the person who needs healing. Jesus even said to the religious leaders of His day that their religious traditions made the Word of God of no effect (Matt. 15:6). This is the reason why it's so important to listen to teaching that is built on the Word of God, and that is anointed by the Holy Spirit. This is how we get hold of revelation that is powerful enough to transform our lives.

- *Political convictions*
  The Kingdom of God doesn't align itself either with the political right or the political left. If we are too loyal to a certain type of politics, this will limit our vision of how the kingdom of God is established in this world through

us. This has become more obvious for me as I have been speaking in many different churches through the years. Some of the leaders within these churches are expressing their political convictions in very vocal ways. Because of this, they're addressing the issues that aligns with their political views, while being either blinded, or even silent on other issues that do not. This creates a limited view of the kingdom of God and it presents a picture of Jesus to the world, that has been hijacked by the preacher's own political worldview. We must realize that the Kingdom of God is not of this world, but the political sphere is part of the world system. Therefore, we need to let the Word of God confront and set us free from false loyalties to the political systems.

Reconnecting to the Mind of Christ

The renewing of the mind is a very liberating process because the mind of Jesus Christ is filled with the creativity of heaven. When our minds are being shaped by His thoughts, we find freedom from the patterns and strongholds that has been tormenting our lives through evil and destructive thoughts. As we have already seen, this is what the mind of Christ looks like:

Finally, brothers and sisters, whatever is true, whatever is honorable, whatever is right, whatever is pure, whatever is lovely, whatever is commendable, if there is any excellence and if anything worthy of praise, think about these things (Phil. 4:8 NASB).

In this passage, Paul is describing what our thought life will look like, as our minds are being renewed. We have been used to think only natural and worldly thoughts, to the degree that it's hard to imagine the freedom we find in living with a mind that has been liberated from fallen thinking. Christlikeness means to think like Christ. When our minds are being renewed:

- We will be thinking more according to the truth.
- We will be thinking more honest thoughts.
- We will have a mind that is being shaped by the justice of God.
- Our minds are being transformed into a stronghold of purity.
- We will be thinking more lovely thoughts.
- We will also be thinking more of things that are of good report, because we will see more of heaven's perspective on reality.

Our minds are being renewed into a place where godly creativity flows, so that we can access heavenly strategies and the solutions that will release the will of God through us. Our life will become much simpler when things like truth, honesty and justice fill our mind. That will make our thoughts a stronghold of God and as a result, our lives will be transformed to reflect the life of Christ.

Accessing the Mind of Christ

Because Jesus now lives within us, we have been given the mind of Christ, so that we can discern the will of God. We have access to His wisdom all the time. In fact, *"it is because of him that you are in Christ Jesus, who has become for us wisdom from God"* (1 Cor. 1:30). God has called us into fellowship with Jesus and it is through that fellowship that we access the wisdom of God, because Jesus Himself is the wisdom of God. I have seen this many times in my life and ministry. I am constantly ministering to a lot of broken people, and dealing with the challenges that ministering to these broken people presents, can at times be very challenging. I have faced a lot of situations throughout the years, where I had no idea how to handle the issues that needed to be dealt with. In these situations, I have learnt not to decide anything until I have peace about what to do. I receive peace as I spend time fellowshipping with Jesus. Abiding in His presence brings a clarity and wisdom, that provides the answers and solutions that I need. I'm very grateful that I don't have to be the smartest guy on the planet to serve God, because I clearly am not. But I do have access to the Father's wisdom through Christ. He is wisdom personified!

Setting Our Minds on Him

Therefore if you have been raised with Christ [to a new life, sharing in His resurrection from the dead], keep seeking the things that are above, where Christ is, seated at the right hand of God. Set your mind and keep focused habitually on the things above [the heavenly things], not on things that are on the earth [which have only temporal value]. For you died [to this world], and your [new, real] life is hidden with Christ in God (Col. 3:1-3 AMP).

We do have full access to the mind of Christ, but manifesting the mind of Christ doesn't happen automatically. We need to make it our daily habit of seek the kingdom of God by setting our mind on heavenly things. This means making it a habit to direct all our attention to Jesus Christ and His presence. He is always with us and He wants us to live in a constant awareness of this. Seeking the kingdom of God first, means to live in fellowship with Jesus. Since He is both Lord and King of the kingdom of God, when we live in fellowship with Him, we are directing our thoughts on the heavenly things. This might sound challenging at first, but when we remember that He is the lover of our soul and our best friend, focusing on Him is a fruit of knowing who He is. This is how we access the heavenly wisdom and how our thinking is renewed to reflect the mind of Christ.

The Natural Man vs. the Spiritual Man

But the natural man receiveth not the things of the Spirit of God: for they are foolishness unto him: neither can he know them, because they are spiritually discerned. But he that is spiritual judgeth all things, yet he himself is judged of no man. For who hath known the mind of the Lord, that he may instruct him? But we have the mind of Christ (1 Cor. 2:14-16).

When Paul writes about the natural man, he describes a person with an unrenewed mind. Such a person is unable to receive the revelations that comes from the Spirit of God. Revelation can't be grasped through the intellect but is discerned by the spirit. The ways of the kingdom of God will always appear to be foolish to the person who doesn't know Jesus. This applies to the believer who still lives with an unrenewed mind as well. Such a believer is still guided by worldly thinking. When Paul writes about the spiritual man, he describes a person who is born again and who has renewed his mind by living in fellowship with Jesus Christ. It is the spiritual man who will receive revelation from the Holy Spirit. Christ is our wisdom and He longs to share His mind with us, so that our thoughts reflect His. This means that our minds are becoming Christlike, which is a good description of the mind that has been liberated and restored by the power of Christ.

Activations

- We read Rom. 12:1-2 and 2 Cor. 10:3-5, earlier in this chapter. Spend some time reflecting on these passages together with the Holy Spirit. Invite Him to give more insight from these two passages, to help you to live in the constant renewal of your mind. Write down what He reveals to you on this topic.

- We saw from Col. 3:1-3 that we're called to habitually set our minds on the things that are above. What does this mean for you? How do you do that consistently? Reflect on this and invite the Holy Spirit to teach and guide you in practicing setting your mind on Christ.

- You have the mind of Christ. Because of this, you have access to divine creativity and heavenly strategies. Take 20-30 minutes in prayer and ask the Father to fill your heart with creative ideas and strategies for how to extend the Kingdom. Write these creative ideas and strategies down.

- Bring the creative ideas and divine strategies that you received to the Father in prayer. Ask Him for concrete steps and an action plan concerning how you can start applying these ideas and strategies. Start taking these steps and apply to this action plan, as soon as possible.

- Spend some time in intercession with the Father. Pray that the body of Christ receives more revelation of the New Covenant, and for our minds to be renewed by a revelation of the Father's heart.

CHAPTER 11: THE FREED AND RESTORED WILL

"For it is [not your strength, but it is] God who is effectively at work in you, both to will and to work [that is, strengthening, energizing, and creating in you the longing and the ability to fulfill your purpose] for His good pleasure" (Phil. 2:13 AMP).

We saw in an earlier chapter that the will of Jesus was completely surrendered and in sync with the will of the Father. Since we are being conformed into His image, this is also the goal for our will. As we're being more rooted and grounded in the Father's love, our will is being liberated so that we can make good choices. This will keep us focused and stable in our walk with the Father. This is possible because Christ lives within us and He provides both longing and ability to do this. We can't break free from the power of sin by trusting in our own choices, since our will is not strong enough to overcome sin. Our part is to surrender our will to the Father and His part is to deliver and restore it. This is the reason that our life with the Father didn't start by us choosing Him, but by Him calling us to Himself. With that calling, He also gave us the ability to respond to Him.

He Chose Us First

None of us possesses a will that is totally free and unaffected by sin. Because every man has been born in a fallen world, all of us have been affected and wounded by sin. This means that the will of every man is in bondage to sin to some degree. Depending on how much someone has yielded to sin or a sinful behavior, that bondage varies in strength. This is the reason that no one is able to come to Christ, except if that person has been drawn there by the Father. When His calling comes, we have freedom to respond to, or resist His invitation.

*Ye have not chosen me, but I have chosen you, and ordained you, that
ye should go and bring forth fruit, and that your fruit should remain:
that whatsoever ye shall ask of the Father in my name, he may give it
you (John 15:16).*

The Father will never stop calling on the lost and He will always
be looking for new ways to reach them. The longing of Jesus is
for everyone to come back home to the Father. Our mission today
is to be partners with Jesus in reaching the world with the gospel.
Since people who aren't born again are still in bondage to sin, we
can't expect them to live according to the laws and values of God.
Therefore, we need to make sure that we're preaching the gospel,
so that every unbeliever can receive Jesus and forgiveness of sins.
It is only when Jesus comes into our life, that real change and the
transformation of our lifestyle can begin.

Chosen to Be Part of His Family

The Father chose us to be part of His family in Christ, even before
He created the world. In his letter to the Ephesians, Paul writes
that *"…according as he hath chosen us in him before the foundation of
the world, that we should be holy and without blame before him in love"*
(Eph. 1:4). This is a powerful revelation, because it shows us that
the Father always wanted us in His family. He has always held a
very special place for every one of us in His heart, and *"…having
predestined us to adoption as sons by Jesus Christ to Himself, according
to the good pleasure of His will, to the praise of the glory of His grace, by
which He made us accepted in the Beloved" (Eph. 1:5-6 NKJV).* The
Father chose us already before He created the world. This means
that He always wanted us to be part of His family. Already long
before any human parent, a friend, or other important people in
our lives rejected us, our Father had already chosen us and made
us accepted in His beloved Son, Jesus Christ. When we see this,
the wounds of abandonment and rejection start to get healed. As
I realized that it was the Father who had chosen me in Christ, I

was set free from all the rejection that used to torment me before. Because my father had abandoned me, I was left with a very deep father-wound in my heart. This wound caused me to accept the lie that I was born to be rejected. I was convinced that there was something wrong with me.

When I realized that the Father had chosen me already before He made the world, something powerful began to shift in my heart. I began receiving His love and approval and as a result, I was healed from the wound of rejection and fatherlessness. The sense of rejection disappeared when I realized that even if people reject me and even though I had completely rejected myself, my Father had always wanted me as His child. This revelation became the beginning of the deliverance and restoration of my will as well. I did nothing to accomplish this. I simply found strength through His grace to break the old, harmful patterns in my life. The Father established new patterns in my life that aligned with His heart.

Our Will Is Empowered by the Grace of God

But by the grace of God I am what I am: and his grace which was bestowed upon me was not in vain; but I laboured more abundantly than they all: yet not I, but the grace of God which was with me (1 Cor. 15:10).

Paul knew that being empowered by the grace of God was his source of strength, that fully enabled him to live as a son of God. It was by that strength he could leave his old life as the religious man he used to be and instead become a pioneering apostle. The same is true for us. Our will is liberated from both the influence and oppression of sin by the empowering grace of God. We need to remember that the grace of God is His active power, working in us. The power of His grace is stronger than sin and it liberates our will, so that we can break free from the influence of all sinful patterns, the world, and the oppression of the devil. It is of vital importance that we understand that the grace of God is an active power at work in our lives. *"And yet, wherever sin increased, there was more than enough of God's grace to triumph all the more! And just as sin reigned through death, so also this sin-conquering grace will reign as king through righteousness, imparting eternal life through Jesus, our Lord and Messiah" (Rom. 5:20-21 TPT).* When we realize that, we find the strength, both to do and be everything that our God has called us to be. All His power and ability are now made available to us through Jesus Christ.

The Example of Paul

Paul is a very good example of the believer who live empowered by the grace of God. He was a very active and hardworking man, but it would be a mistake to think of his accomplishments as the result of him leaning on his own strength. Paul became strong in God, because of the grace of God that empowered Him. Grace is also God's unmerited favor. Paul was favored and empowered by God's grace. Doors to preach the gospel and to plant churches opened for him in a supernatural way because of God's favor. It was in this way that Paul walked in wisdom and anointing from God, to establish the believers in their identity in Christ.

The mystery in a nutshell is just this: Christ is in you, so therefore you can look forward to sharing in God's glory. It's that simple. That is the substance of our Message. We preach Christ, warning people not to add to the Message. We teach in a spirit of profound common sense so that we can bring each person to maturity. To be mature is to be basic. Christ! No more, no less. That's what I'm working so hard at day after day, year after year, doing my best with the energy God so generously gives me (Col. 1:27-29 The Message).

When Paul was preaching, He always preached Christ and Him crucified (1 Cor. 2:1-5). That was his response to every challenge that the churches he had planted were facing. He knew that true change is only possible by abiding in the love of the Father. Paul found all his motivation and strength, from the energy that the Father so generously provided to him. This is a very good way to describe how the grace of God operated through his ministry.

This has been my experience as well. While writing this chapter I'm in Helsinki, the capital of Finland, teaching at a Bible school as well as preaching in several evening services. I already knew many years ago that I was called to minister in Finland, but I had no contacts there at all. Neither did I know anything about how to build an itinerant ministry. One day, while I was pastoring at a church in the north of Sweden, the Father spoke to me and said: "I'm releasing you into itinerant ministry. You will travel all over the world and bring my healing power to the body of Christ". As I was released into that assignment, a whole new level of favor and empowerment from God came upon my life. This favor gave me open doors to travel to the nations. Since then, I have been to Finland many times and I have many more future trips planned. I couldn't make this happen, but as I yielded to the grace of God, He empowered me to walk in the calling He had given me. When we yield our will to Christ, He empowers us to make the choices needed to become everything that He has called us to be.

Surrender to Christ Will Become Our Lifestyle

In the same way that Jesus humbled Himself and made the will of God the focus of His life, submitting to the Father will become our lifestyle as well. As our lives are being shaped by the love of the Father, it will always be a representation of the life of Christ. When we read about the life of Jesus in the Bible, we are reading the story of our lives as well. Paul summarizes the direction of the life of every believer, by pointing us to the way of Jesus:

You must have the same attitude that Christ Jesus had. Though he was God, he did not think of equality with God as something to cling to.

Instead, he gave up his divine privileges; he took the humble position of a slave and was born as a human being. When he appeared in human form, he humbled himself in obedience to God and died a criminal's death on a cross (Phil. 2:5-8 NLT).

Of course, there are important differences between our lives and the life that Jesus lived. We don't have to die on a cross to redeem the world. Instead, we're reaping all the benefits of His suffering. The way in which our lives will be a representation of the life of Christ is that we will live with the same attitude of humility and availability to the Father. As our will is being liberated from the power of sin and the influence of the world, we become free to give up control over our lives, by surrendering to the will of the Father. It's important to remember that being conformed into the image of Christ is a lifelong process and the Father is very patient with us. His love conquers our hearts one area at a time. Learning to abide in the love of God, in a way that sets us free to follow Him wherever He is leading is a process that will take time, but the fruit of walking through this process is worth it!

The Damaged Will

There are some signs to look for, that show us that our will needs to be healed and restored. I have listed a few of them here below. These are not clear cut, in the sense that you will recognize only one of them at a time. They often overlap and being set free takes time. It's only by living in a deep fellowship with the Father that we find lasting freedom. He is not in a hurry. He leads us gently at a pace we can handle. Here's a list which contains some points that reveals how an oppressed will might look like:

- *A will in bondage*
  We can recognize that our will is in bondage, if we want to make good choices but are unable to make them. Paul describes how that looks like in his letter to the Romans,

where he revealed his personal struggles with this, in his former life as a Pharisee (Rom. 7:14-25). Paul is referring to his life as a non-believer in this text, which means that He is describing the state of an unregenerate person, but this is the experience of a believer whose will has not yet been liberated by God as well. Our will is only liberated and freed from the power of sin by the grace of Christ. Sometimes, a person we minister to might need to be set free from bondages of sinful patterns, if they are to be set free to make good choices. The most important step if we want to get free is to surrender our will to the Father. As His love and grace operate within our will, the bondages will weaken until they break and freedom is established.

- *A broken will*

  If someone has failed multiple times to fulfill a dream, or to reach a certain goal, they can become so disillusioned that they just give up. Their will has been broken. This is a very painful experience. Losing hope to find a positive change for a better future can break the will and lead us to passivity. Proverbs states that *"where there is no vision, the people perish" (Prov. 29:18)*. It also says that *"a merry heart doeth good like a medicine: But a broken spirit drieth the bones" (Prov. 17:22)*. Having a broken spirit is the perfect description of a person whose will is broken. We find an example of this in the gospel of John, where the apostle writes about the man who had been lame for thirty-eight long years (John 5:1-15). This man longed to be healed, but because he couldn't move, other people were able to jump into the pool of Bethesda before he had the chance. The will of this man was broken by the disappointments he had faced through the years, but Jesus had a solution: *"Jesus saith unto him, Rise, take up thy bed, and walk. And immediately the man was made whole, and took up his bed, and walked: and on the same day was the sabbath (John 5:8-9).*

This is a powerful illustration of how the grace of God empowers us to make godly choices. When we have lost our courage, we need to reconnect with the Father's love because His *"...love bears all things, believes all things, hopes all things, endures all things. Love never fails"* (1 Cor. 13:7-8 *NKJV*). The Father's love will revive every lost vision and restore all our broken dreams.

- *A passive will*

   Passivity is built on the false assumption that it is more secure to continue the way it has always been. A person in this place would prefer to not make any choices at all, because doing so is too uncomfortable and demanding. Such a person has partnered with the spirit of death and needs to be called out of the grave, to be set free from the bondages of passivity and fear. Because we are in Christ, we are overcomers and we can live in total freedom and victory, no matter what goes on around us (Rom. 8:37). We are delivered from passivity by understanding that making good choices is not a threat to our well-being or safety. God has called us to live a dynamic life with Him. When we encounter the Father's heart, our dreams are ignited and we can take new steps into freedom. When we start to make good choices, we will realize that being empowered to make good choices opens life for us in a major way. Our possibilities are endless when we walk with God.

- *A will that is controlled by false loyalties*

   Sometimes we do not realize how much the people we have in our lives affect us. Solomon took wives from the people that God had told Israel to stay away from. They turned his heart away to follow other gods. *"For it came to pass, when Solomon was old, that his wives turned away his heart after other gods: and his heart was not perfect with the LORD his God, as was the heart of David his father" (1 Kings 11:4).* I have watched many people miss what God had planned for them, simply because they allowed the wrong people kind of people too influence their lives. It hindered them from living fully in the will of God. When this is the case, our relationships need new boundaries, so that all the ungodly influence is removed. Relatives, friends, or even our closest family members are not more important than the will of God. It is good to steward our relationships well, but we need to make sure to stay free from ungodly influences (Mark. 3:31-34). We should be intentional in cultivating relationships that empower us to fulfill the call of God (Prov. 15:22, 19:20).

- ***A will that is oppressed by demons.***
If we have opened up for destructive spiritual influence, our will can be oppressed by demons. The most common way that this happens, is either through sin or wounds, that haven't yet been healed. Living in sin, or a failure to deal with the pain of the past opens the door for spiritual oppression. As we have seen earlier in this book, demons cannot access our lives whenever they want. They must gain legal right to do so. We can usually discern demonic oppression by observing what it is that drives a person. The man in the country of Gadarenes didn't want to live in the wilderness, but he was driven there by demonic powers (Luke 8:29-36). These demons had a strong grip of this man but couldn't control him completely. He was still able to come to Jesus. The Lord set him free and he returned to a normal state of mind once again. *"Then they went out to see what was done; and came to Jesus, and found the man, out of whom the devils were departed, sitting at the feet of Jesus, clothed, and in his right mind: and they were afraid" (Luke 8:35).* This man was totally transformed. He became an evangelist, who preached Christ by giving his

testimony everywhere (Luke 8:38-39). The person whose will is bound by demons needs to be delivered. This can happen through prayer and by encountering the love of the Father. Demons can't stand the love of the Father and when the person who is oppressed by demons learn how to abide in His love, that person will usually be delivered from demonic bondages as well. Prayer and counseling might also be needed to find lasting freedom.

- *A will that has been deceived by religion*
  Religious teaching and legalism will limit the capacity to make good choices as well. Our good choice is based on revelation, but religion always paints a distorted picture of God. If we fail to see the plan that He has for our lives, we will not be able to make choices to align with it. If we believe that God is using sickness or poverty to teach us something, it is much harder to believe that He wants to heal us and bless our finances. We need to receive fresh revelation from the Holy Spirit every day, so that we can grow in the love of the Father. Revelation helps us to stay fresh in our relationship with Him and it empower us to activate our will to make good choices. This is the reason that Paul encouraged us to guard our freedom in Christ, by making sure that we don't go back under the religious burdens of legalistic teachings (Gal. 5:1-2).

These are some examples of a damaged and oppressed will. It is obvious that a damaged will looks different for different people, depending on our personalities, culture and other circumstances, but the solution is always the same: Learning to abide in the love of the Father.

The Father's Love is the Cure

The symptoms of a damaged will are many, but the restoration of the will is always found in the Father's love. This is important to remember. We don't need to look for signs of a damaged will, or try to find the problems by ourselves. Our focus should be on knowing the Father. If He wants to, He will show us the issues to deal with. As we abide in His love, we find freedom to make good choices. His love, that delivers, heals, and restores our will, now lives inside of us, so we have already taken the cure.

"I have revealed to them who you are and I will continue to make you even more real to them, so that they may experience the same endless love that you have for me, for your love will now live in them, even as I live in them" (John 17:26 TPT).

It might take time for us to see the full manifestation of His love within us, but we are on our way. It is fairly obvious that most of us are not yet where we want to be, but neither are we the same person that we were last year. The Father is working in us. We are always "work in progress", but eventually we will become everything that He has called us to be. A huge part of growing in His purposes is to live with a freed and restored will.

<h1 style="text-align:center">Activations</h1>

- We studied Phil. 2:12-13 and John 15:16, earlier in this chapter. Spend some time reflecting on these passages together with the Holy Spirit. Invite Him to give more insights from these passages to show you how to fully surrender your will to the Father. Write down the new insights that He reveals to you.

- Surrendering our will to the Father will always be the first step into a lifestyle that reflects the life of Christ. This lifestyle is portrayed in Phil. 2:1-10. Read these verses together with the Holy Spirit. Ask Him to give more revelation on a Christlike life from this passage. Write down the insights you receive.

- Within this chapter, I wrote a list which describe some symptoms of the will that has been damaged by sin. Here are the states of the damaged will from that list:

  1. *A will in bondage*
  2. *A Broken Will*
  3. *A Passive Will*
  4. *A Will that is Controlled by False Loyalties*
  5. *A Will that is Oppressed by Demons*
  6. *A Will that has Been Deceived by Religion*

  Do you recognize any of these symptoms in your will? Have you ever needed deliverance in the area of your will? Reflect on this and ask the Holy Spirit to reveal more on the state of your will. Ask him specifically to reveal areas of bondage and damage in your will.

- Take 20-30 minutes in prayer. Ask the Father to pour His love into your will. Also, ask Him to deliver and restore your will from all oppression and damage, so that it can fully reflect the will of Christ.

- We have seen how Jesus was free to always make the right choices. He could do this because He always did what he saw the Father doing. Ask the Father to give you wisdom to discern His will and to strengthen you to make wise choices in life.

CHAPTER 12: A RICH AND BALANCED EMOTIONAL LIFE

But the fruit produced by the Holy Spirit within you is divine love in all its varied expressions: joy that overflows, peace that subdues, patience that endures, kindness in action, a life full of virtue, faith that prevails, gentleness of heart, and strength of spirit. Never set the law above these qualities, for they are meant to be limitless (Gal 5:22-23 TPT).

As we have already seen, Jesus has a very rich emotional life and, in the gospels, we can read about how He expressed a wide array of emotions. Jesus could do that because His emotional life rested on the secure foundation of the fruit of the Spirit. The fruit of the Spirit is one fruit, but its expressions are many. That fruit is love and it grows within us, when we abide in the Father's love. The good news is that His love has now been poured into our hearts through the Holy Spirit. Everything that we want to impart into other people of spiritual value, we must first have received from God ourselves. The same is true when speaking of the fruit of the Spirit. The fruit of the Spirit is produced within us, when we stay rooted in the heart of the Father. This fruit is expressed in the following ways:

1. *Divine love in all its varied expressions*
2. *Joy that overflows*
3. *Peace that subdues*
4. *Patience that endures*
5. *Kindness in action*
6. *A life full of virtue*
7. *Faith that prevails*
8. *Gentleness of heart*
9. *Strength of spirit*

It is important to remember that we are talking about the fruit of the Spirit here. We are not talking about performing in the Spirit, or the disciplined life of the believer. Discipline and good works will be the result of the fruit of the Spirit growing in our lives, but the only way for this fruit to grow is when we're living in an intimate fellowship with Jesus. It can't be produced in our lives by religious efforts. In fact, legalism is helpless to bring about the fruit of the Spirit. It will stir up the works of the flesh. *"Legalism is helpless in bringing this about; it only gets in the way. Among those who belong to Christ, everything connected with getting our own way and mindlessly responding to what everyone else calls necessities is killed off for good—crucified" (Gal. 5:23-24 The Message).*

We have now been crucified with Christ, so our lives can only be transformed by us allowing Christ to live His life through us. We have been delivered from religious performance by dying to the law with Jesus Christ, and we have now been raised to a new life where we live by His life. He is our sanctification and the source of a godly life. Paul is making the following statement on this:

I have been crucified with Christ; it is no longer I who live, but Christ lives in me; and the life which I now live in the flesh I live by faith in the Son of God, who loved me and gave Himself for me. I do not set aside the grace of God; for if righteousness comes through the law, then Christ died in vain (Gal. 2:20-21 NKJV).

Christ has become our life and through Him, we become rooted and grounded in the love of the Father. This is the only way that we can find lasting freedom and restoration in our emotional life.

Wounded Emotions

When we have a balanced and healthy emotional life, then all our emotions will express the fruit of the spirit. Joy, peace, and love will be the main state of our emotional lives. If we have unhealed wounds in our hearts, they will manifest as toxic emotions. For example, if a person has been hurt in an important relationship and that hurt grows into disappointment, the emotional life will be colored by bitterness and anger. When we have pain in certain areas of life it means that we need healing. I'm not indicating that whenever we feel pain there is something wrong in us, but if the pain stays in our heart, it's an indication that there are wounds that needs to be healed. It is important that we learn how to listen to the message that our emotions communicate to us, since they reveal the state of the heart.

It is a good thing to realize that we need some emotional healing. That is the first step to being healed. When we're recognizing the pain within our hearts, we can run to the Father and find healing. When I notice that I need healing within my heart, I have learned to take that as an invitation to go deeper into the Father's love, by handing the areas of pain to Him. Painful emotions are never our enemy. They simply reveal the wounded areas in our heart. This is a good thing, since it helps us to find the real root of the problem, so that we can invite the Holy Spirit to minister to us in that area.

Our Emotions Are Delivered and Restored by the Love of the Father

And we have known and believed the love that God has for us. God is love, and he who abides in love abides in God, and God in him. Love has been perfected among us in this: that we may have boldness in the day of judgment; because as He is, so are we in this world. There is no fear in love; but perfect love casts out fear, because fear involves torment. But he who fears has not been made perfect in love. We love Him because He first loved us (1 John 4:16-19 NKJV).

As we have already seen, the fruit of the Spirit is produced in our lives when we abide in the love of the Father. It is impossible not to love people and to grow in the fruit of the Spirit, when we are rooted and grounded in the love of Christ. Our emotions will not be transformed by our choices. Our choices are connected to the will, not the emotions. You can make good choices with a broken emotional life but if we live like that, we will end up fighting our emotions all the time and that is not why God gave us emotions. Our emotions are meant to express the love of the Father, but we are also relational beings, who have been created with a need for deep and meaningful connections. This is why our emotions are so important. A huge part of how of our deep relationships are formed, happens on an emotional level. As we have already seen, emotions are not our enemies and if our emotional life has been damaged, God wants us to be healed. We should not ignore our emotions and neither should we consider them as the problem. We simply need to invite the Holy Spirit to fill our emotional life with His presence and the love of the Father. That will bring transformation so that we can live with a rich emotional life that is built on the foundation of the fruit of the Spirit.

A Wonderful Breakthrough

I experienced a powerful breakthrough in this area that has been crucial to my growth in the Father's love. I had received a lot of teaching concerning how to handle my emotions that wasn't at all helpful to me. The point of this teaching was that I should be walking in faith and not listen to my emotions at all. This led to me trying to ignore my feelings. Since I had a lot of brokenness in my life, there was a lot of pain hidden deep in my heart. These emotions that I was ignoring, tried to communicate that I needed to deal with the root of the problem, but because I ignored these signals, I became filled with both anxiety, fear and depression. I didn't know what to do about is, so I ended up denying that I even needed healing. This caused me to live very unauthentically and I pretended that this pain was not there. When I finally did realize that walking by faith is not a contradiction to being honest with my feelings, I found a much healthier way to manage my inner world. In fact, it is a powerful expression of faith to dare to be vulnerable and open before God. I gave the Holy Spirit access to the pains that I had buried deep inside of my heart. I received a lot of deliverance and deep healing in my emotional life. When I surrendered my pain to the Father, His love started to pour into my emotions and the wounds within my heart started to heal. I discovered that I no longer needed to fight against my emotions. I became more stable and I could see how the fruit of the Spirit was growing in my life. This growth isn't always as quick or as painless as I had hoped it to be, but it's happening one step at the time. As we're experiencing transformation in our emotional life, our feelings will reflect the emotions of Jesus Christ.

A Clarification

There are times when we must ignore our feelings. Sometimes, doing what is right doesn't feel good. It is not always pleasant to walk in obedience to the Father, or to sacrifice, time, money, and strength to help a friend in need, even though we know it is the right thing to do. In times like that, we need to make the choice to love people anyway. The point is that when our emotional life has been damaged, our feelings has lost the ability to express the fruit of the Spirit. That will lead to a constant battle and struggle as we live in the will of Christ. That is not how we are created to live. Our inner life should be in harmony with the will of God so that our whole being, including our emotions expresses the heart of the Father and the fruit of the Spirit.

Activations

- We studied Gal. 5:22-23, earlier in this chapter. Spend some time reflecting on this passage together with the Holy Spirit. Reflect on the fruit of the Spirit, using the Passion Translation and one other translation. Invite Him to give more revelation from this passage, to help you fully surrender your emotional life to the Father. Write down any new insights that He reveals to you.

- Surrender your emotions to the Father. Ask Him to fill your emotions with His love and the fruit of the Spirit. Ask Jesus to transform your emotions, so that you can fully reflect and reveal Jesus in this area.

- Take 20-30 minutes in prayer. Invite the Holy Spirit to reveal any emotional wound within your heart. Then write down what He shows you. Ask Him to pour the Father's love into these wounds. Spend some time just soaking in the healing love of the Father.

- Here is a list of the fruit of the Spirit. Ask the Father to fill the areas within your heart with this fruit. Use this list in prayer and ask the Father to fill your emotions with an abundance of these expressions of His love:

  1. *Divine love in all its varied expressions*
  2. *Joy that overflows*
  3. *Peace that subdues*
  4. *Patience that endures*
  5. *Kindness in action*
  6. *A life full of virtue*
  7. *Faith that prevails*
  8. *Gentleness of heart*
  9. *Strength of spirit*

CHAPTER 13: A CLEAN CONSCIENCE BEFORE GOD

"And Paul, earnestly beholding the council, said, Men and brethren, I have lived in all good conscience before God until this day. And the high priest Ananias commanded them that stood by him to smite him on the mouth" (Acts 23:1-2).

Another area that is transformed by the love of the Father, is our conscience. When His love starts to cleanse our conscience, it will confront the very root of religion. All religion is always fueled by guilt and condemnation, both of which will defile the conscience. This is the reason the high priest became so angry when Paul said that he always had lived with a clean conscience before God. It's inconceivable to the religious mindset that it is possible to live in unbroken union with Christ, with a clean conscience. Yet, a clean conscience is part of our inheritance as children of God.

What Is the Conscience?

A very simple definition of the conscience is that it is the internal instrument that God has given us to communicate with the Holy Spirit and be sensitive to His guidance. Learning to listen to our conscience is how we define and guard our personal boundaries. The Father has given us the conscience as an instrument, through which we are convicted of sins. Since these are the function of the conscience, it is not hard to imagine the problems we get when it is defiled. When our conscience becomes seared or hardened, it will no longer function as God has planned. It will either become too sensitive, leading to an internal life that is tormented by false guilt. Or the voice of the conscience will be silenced in such a way that our heart become hardened. We will look at the bad fruits of a damaged conscience in a moment, but first we need to look at how our conscience gets defiled. Even more important, we need to look at how our conscience is totally cleansed and restored by the blood of Jesus.

The Blood of Christ Purifies the Conscience

Therefore, brethren, having boldness to enter the Holiest by the blood of Jesus, by a new and living way which He consecrated for us, through the veil, that is, His flesh, and having a High Priest over the house of God, let us draw near with a true heart in full assurance of faith, having our hearts sprinkled from an evil conscience and our bodies washed with pure water (Hebr. 10:19-22 NKJV).

Jesus opened a new and living way for us to the Father, through His redemptive work on the cross. We can now abide in His love and presence with boldness. This is all because the blood of Jesus has opened the way for us. We have been cleansed and sanctified and we have a constant and instant access to the throne of grace, but for us to relate to the Father with boldness and full assurance of faith, our conscience needs to be cleansed and made whole. We can't fix the conscience by ourselves, but the Father has made this possible through Jesus Christ. We find the answer to how He did that in the following passage:

For if the blood of bulls and of goats, and the ashes of an heifer sprinkling the unclean, sanctifieth to the purifying of the flesh: how much more shall the blood of Christ, who through the eternal Spirit offered himself without spot to God, purge your conscience from dead works to serve the living God? (Hebr. 9:13-14)

Our conscience is cleansed when we get a revelation of the blood of Christ. Through His blood, our sins have been washed away and through the blood, every accusation of the devil have been silenced (Rev. 12:10-11). All our sins — past, present, and future — have already been punished and carried away through Christ. Every accusation against us has now been nailed to the cross and is nullified. A revelation of the blood of Jesus delivers us from all our sin consciousness, so that we can live with full assurance that we are the righteousness of God in Christ. It is by a revelation of the blood of Jesus that our conscience is cleansed and restored. It can then begin to operate in the way that our Father intended.

What Are Dead Works?

We read that the blood of Christ purifies our conscience from all our dead works. Dead works are works that we do to please God, based on guilt and condemnation. When we forget who we are in Christ, or what Jesus did for us on the cross, we easily fall into the trap of doing dead works. A dead work is not defined as such by the act itself, but by the motives behind it. The Bible also talks about the works of faith, which are pleasing to God (Jam. 2:18-26). The difference between dead works and the works of faith, lies in the motive behind the action. If I do certain things to make God look upon me in a more favorable way, that is what the Bible calls dead works. If I instead do something as a response to His love, then that act is an act of faith.

A Seared Conscience

But the Spirit explicitly says that in later times some will fall away from the faith, paying attention to deceitful spirits and teachings of demons, by means of the hypocrisy of liars seared in their own conscience as with a branding iron, who forbid marriage and advocate abstaining from foods which God has created to be gratefully shared in by those who believe and know the truth. For everything created by God is good, and nothing is to be rejected if it is received with gratitude; for it is sanctified by means of the word of God and prayer (1 Tim. 4:1-5 NASB).

Paul uses the expression *"seared with a hot iron"*, when describing a conscience that has been hardened. Usually, when I ask people to describe a seared conscience, they think of someone who lives a worldly lifestyle and who doesn't care about the Father's will, but that is not the type of person that Paul is describing here. The people he is referring to, were so committed to the Lord that they abstained from marrying and eating food that they considered to be unclean. In other words, these people became more religious when their conscience was seared, but their seal for God was not built on the finished work of Christ. It was instead driven by guilt and religion. Paul shows us that God has created both food and marriage, as gifts for us to enjoy. Everything is sanctified through the Word of God and prayer. As we're finding our true freedom in Christ, we will become more and more grateful to Jesus, for all the wonderful gifts He has given us by giving us life.

The Accuser Has Been Silenced by the Blood of Christ

Then God made you alive with Christ, for he forgave all our sins. He canceled the record of the charges against us and took it away by nailing it to the cross. In this way, he disarmed the spiritual rulers and authorities. He shamed them publicly by his victory over them on the cross (Col. 2: 13-15 NLT).

Before Jesus died on the cross, the devil had legal right to accuse and oppress us, because of the sins we had committed. But now our debt has been cancelled and Jesus has carried away our sins. Therefore, the accuser no longer has any valid accusations at all, to hold against us before God. The only way he can operate now is by deception, lying by telling us that we are still condemned and that we need to try to please God.

If he succeeds, our conscience becomes seared and we will end up trying to please God through dead works. Through the years, I have become better at recognizing when I'm about to fall in this trap by the inner numbness and heaviness that follow. When I find that legalism has crept into my heart, I have learned that it is time to get a much deeper revelation of the blood of Jesus. I do this by spending time with Jesus, meditating on Scriptures about the blood and by listening to good teaching. This help me to keep my focus on Jesus.

What Is the Fruit of a Bad Conscience?

To understand why it is so important to have a clean conscience before the Father, we are now going to look at the fruit of a seared and defiled conscience. The contrast between them clearly shows how different our life with the Father becomes, if our conscience is liberated and cleansed. As we're doing this, let's remember the functions of the conscience. These are the destructive fruits of the defiled conscience:

- *We will be tormented by false guilt.*
- *We will confuse the guidance of the Holy Spirit, with religious accusation and condemnation.*
- *We will be confused when it comes to our personal boundaries. Consequently, we will not be able to guard them. Because of this our boundaries will be overstepped.*
- *We will lack boldness in our prayer life.*
- *We will not be able to live out of who we are in Christ.*
- *We will have no boldness in our witness and service to man.*

The Liberated Conscience

As we have already seen, our conscience is purified by the blood of Christ. This happens when we get a revelation of the spiritual reality that the blood represents. Because Jesus succeeded in His redemptive work, we never need to live under condemnation or guilt again. *"Therefore there is now no condemnation at all for those who are in Christ Jesus"* (Rom. 8:1 NASB). Our lives become full of boldness and freedom when our conscience is cleansed. Here are some of the powerful benefits of a clean conscience:

- *We will live with an awareness of our righteousness in Christ, and we will be established in our identity as sons and daughters of God.*
- *We will be able to clearly discern the leading of the Holy Spirit.*
- *We will be able to define and guard personal boundaries.*
- *We will have boldness in approaching the Father, which will lead to a powerful and effective prayer life.*
- *We will be able to serve people with a boldness that is the fruit of a bold and intimate relationship with God.*

The Conscience and Personal Freedom

"I know and am convinced in the Lord Jesus that nothing is unclean in itself; but to the one who thinks something is unclean, to that person it is unclean. For if because of food your brother or sister is hurt, you are no longer walking in accordance with love" (Rom. 14:14-15 NASB).

There are many things in life that can't really be defined as sinful, or pure in themselves. Things like music, movies, entertainment, or hobbies fall into this category. The Bible tells us how to think and to make wise decisions when handling the grey areas of life, but it doesn't give us very specific instructions. This is when it's important to have a sound conscience, since our choices in these matters come down to personal boundaries. People are different and we can be affected differently by different things. This means that for some it might be no problem to listen to secular music or the radio, while others would feel uncomfortable with that. Some of us might be fine with watching sports or movies on TV, while others are not. What is right or wrong in these matters cannot be determined by a universal standard, but by personal boundaries. Paul had to deal with this several times. One huge thing was the food and meat that had been offered to idols. He had to address this issue several times in his letters.

The Conscience of Our Brothers and Sisters

However, there is not in everyone that knowledge; for some, with consciousness of the idol, until now eat it as a thing offered to an idol; and their conscience, being weak, is defiled. But food does not commend us to God; for neither if we eat are we the better, nor if we do not eat are we the worse. But beware lest somehow this liberty of yours become a stumbling block to those who are weak. For if anyone sees you who have knowledge eating in an idol's temple, will not the conscience of him who is weak be emboldened to eat those things offered to idols? And because of your knowledge shall the weak brother perish, for whom Christ died? But when you thus sin against the brethren, and wound their weak conscience, you sin against Christ. Therefore, if food makes my brother stumble, I will never again eat meat, lest I make my brother stumble (1 Cor. 8:7-13 NKJV).

As children of God, we have freedom to both define and protect our boundaries in the grey areas of life, together with our Father. No one has the right or authority to impose their own standards, or convictions, upon another believer in these matters. The only time we are encouraged to restrain our personal freedom is when we spend time with other believers that might stumble because of us. In such cases, loving and honoring them is more important than insisting upon our freedom. In the kingdom of God, loving and building one another up is always more important than our own personal rights. There are things that I like, but that some of my friends have problems with. When I spend time with them, I restrain my freedom because they are more important to me. My personal freedom is important but building up the church in love is even more important.

A Clean Conscience Is Part of Our Inheritance in Christ

A clean conscience is one of the major blessings that is included in our inheritance as children of God. I have seen how numerous people have received powerful breakthrough and freedom when their conscience has been cleansed by the blood of Jesus. To have our conscience purified by His blood, will be the start of healing and restoration in many areas of life. This is because once we get a revelation of the blood of Jesus, it reveals our identity in Christ in a powerful way. This has been true in my own life, but also in the lives of the many people that I have ministered to throughout the years. It's an amazing freedom to live with a clean conscience, being aware of our righteousness in Christ and to live in a bold relationship with our heavenly Father. This is our inheritance!

Activations

- We studied Hebr. 9:13-14 and 10:19-22 in this chapter. Spend some time reflecting on these passages with the Holy Spirit. Invite Him to provide more insights from these passages, so that your conscience can be set free and cleansed from dead works. Write down what He reveals to you.

- We read about a seared conscience and the doctrine of demons from 1 Tim. 4:1-5. Read this passage with the Holy Spirit and invite Him to provide more revelation on this topic. What are these demonic doctrines? What does it mean to have a seared conscience? Write down your discoveries and revelations.

- We have seen how religion and legalism damages our conscience. Why is religion and legalism so unhealthy for our conscience? How can you recognize that your conscience has been seared by doctrines of demons? Invite Jesus to speak to you on this topic. Write down the new insights that you receive.

- Take 20-30 minutes in prayer. Invite Jesus to minister to your conscience by cleansing it with His blood. Ask the Father to fill your conscience with His love, so that it becomes sensitive and open to the voice of the Holy Spirit.

CHAPTER 14: DELIVERED FROM GENERATIONAL SINS

For you know that it was not with perishable things such as silver or gold that you were redeemed from the empty way of life handed down to you from your ancestors, but with the precious blood of Christ, a lamb without blemish or defect (1 Pet. 1:18-19 NIV).

When we were delivered from the power of sin through Christ, the power of all the sinful inheritances and patterns, that we had inherited from our parents and earlier generations were broken. Every family line has been damaged by sin in certain ways. This has created sinful patterns that have been passed along through the generations. These patterns are called generational curses, or generational sins. A simple way of describing what generational curses is, would be that they are broken and sinful characteristics which has been passed down to us through the generational lines by our parents. These patterns have then become character traits in our families. Examples of such characteristics could be:

- Addictions
- Fear and anxiety
- Depression
- Sexual sins
- Poverty and slave mentality
- Prejudices against certain nations, classes, or people in authority

There are natural explanations to how this happens. We have all been shaped by our environment and the people that have had a strong influence on us. Our parents have usually influenced and shaped our lives more than anyone else. That influence includes the passing on of habits and values to us. We need to understand that there are also spiritual realities behind this, which is familiar spirits and the power of sin. I often meet people who express that they have been unable to break free from their sinful inheritance, which they have received from earlier generations. The gospel is good news for everyone in bondage. There is both freedom and a much better inheritance for us in Christ.

Jesus came to set all the captives free and to destroy the works of the devil (1 John 3:8). When we died to our sins with Christ, we were delivered from the power of generational sins as well (Rom. 6:1-11). Sometimes, deliverance from these generational sins will happen by simply listening when the truth of the gospel is being proclaimed. After all, the gospel is the power of God to salvation for us who believe (Rom. 1:16-17). Sometimes, these generational curses are broken through prayer and repentance. Jesus reversed every curse and undid the power of every sinful pattern through the cross. There is a now way to freedom for all of us!

Generational Curses and the Old Covenant

You shall not make for yourself an image in the form of anything in heaven above or on the earth beneath or in the waters below. You shall not bow down to them or worship them; for I, the Lord your God, am a jealous God, punishing the children for the sin of the parents to the third and fourth generation of those who hate me, but showing love to a thousand generations of those who love me and keep my commandments (Exodus 20:4-6 NIV).

In the Old Covenant, there are many scriptures on how sins like idolatry, not only affected the people who were worshipping the false gods, but the coming generations as well (see also Exo. 34:7, Num. 14:18, Deut. 5:9). This happened because the people didn't obey the law. The consequences of disobedience to the law, were what Paul calls *"the curse of the law"* (Gal. 3:13). The reason that this happens is that a sinful lifestyle opens the door for the devil to bind family lines in sinful patterns. Yet, we can see that this was never God's heart for His people:

"The soul who sins shall die. The son shall not bear the guilt of the father, nor the father bear the guilt of the son. The righteousness of the righteous shall be upon himself, and the wickedness of the wicked shall be upon himself" (Ezek. 18:20 NKJV).

The Lord never wanted it to be this way, which several passages in the Old Testament clearly reveal (see Deut. 24:16, Jer. 31:29-30, Ezek. 18:1-4). However, because the people of God chose to relate to Him through a covenant of works, generational curses became one of the results. When the Bible speaks about God visiting the iniquity of the fathers upon the children, it is not speaking about the Father actively punishing them for the sins of their ancestors. It means that when a person in covenant with God sinned, God removed the protection from that area of his life, so that the devil could build a stronghold there. In other words, God handed the people over to their own sinful behavior, but there was still a way out of of generational curses already in the Old Covenant.

But if they confess their wrongdoing and the wrongdoing of their forefathers, in their unfaithfulness which they committed against Me, and also in their acting with hostility against Me— I also was acting with hostility against them, to bring them into the land of their enemies—or if their uncircumcised heart is humbled so that they then make amends for their wrongdoing, then I will remember My covenant with Jacob, and I will remember also My covenant with Isaac, and My covenant with Abraham as well, and I will remember the land. (Lev. 26:39-42 NASB)

As always, the way out of being oppressed by sin, was humility and repentance. This reveals that God never wanted His children to be oppressed by generational sins. Instead, He provided a way out. In the New Covenant, the way out from generational sins is much better. When Jesus died on the cross, everything changed and no curse has the right to torment us anymore.

Jesus Has Broken and Reversed Every Curse

Christ hath redeemed us from the curse of the law, being made a curse for us: for it is written, cursed is every one that hangeth on a tree: that the blessing of Abraham might come on the Gentiles through Jesus Christ; that we might receive the promise of the Spirit through faith (Gal 3:13-14).

We don't have to be stuck within the sinful patterns of the former generations anymore. Christ took every generational curse upon Himself on the cross. The punishment for every sin that we have ever committed, was placed upon Jesus. He released us from the patterns of generational sins. He was made a curse for us and we can no longer be cursed. We are blessed children (Eph. 1:3). Our generational inheritance is the Kingdom of God and the blessing of Abraham. Sometimes, I talk to believers who are afraid of the power of generational curses and they seem to think that it must be a hard struggle for them to get free. The truth is that the battle is over and Jesus has won. Jesus has reversed every curse and we have been set free by the power of the cross. We cannot be cursed anymore. Because of the finished work of Jesus Christ there is no longer any foundation for generational curses to work within our lives anymore. This is the reason that Proverbs declares: *"Like a flitting sparrow, like a flying swallow, So a curse without cause shall not alight"* (Prov. 26:2).

I Was Delivered from Generational Sins

I have personal experience of being delivered from generational curses. This has affected my life in a powerful way. One of these generational curses was a big stronghold of fear and anxiety. The other stronghold, which was closely related to fear could maybe best be described as impossibility thinking. I was delivered from the stronghold of fear, when I realized that fear isn't my friend. I had almost made fear and anxiety a place of refuge and comfort, but as I came to know the Father's love, it became clear to me that this stronghold was a huge problem in my life. I took a couple of days in prayer, renouncing these very strongholds. I realized that they had no power over me anymore. I saw in the Scriptures that I'm now dead to sin, but alive to God (Rom. 6:11).

My new family tree is in Christ and I have a new identity in Him. In the family of Christ, there is no fear or anxiety. Instead, we live in the fullness of the Father's love which drives out all fear. We possess the peace of heaven, which delivers us from all anxiety. When I applied this revelation in prayer, a dramatic change took place within me. All fear and anxiety disappeared from my life. I found strength in the Father's love and by the peace that I found in Christ instead. That was a major upgrade!

I was delivered from impossibility thinking as well. This kind of thinking had created the assumption in me that it was impossible to fulfill my dreams, or to reach any of the goals I had for my life. I was delivered from this diabolic stronghold, by spending time with some friends and leaders that are both possibility thinkers and visionaries. By spending time with these friends, I began to realize how limited I was in my thinking. I discovered that this was a major hindrance to fulfilling God's plan for me. Over time, the possibility thinking and visionary mindset that these friends had cultivated by co-laboring with God, was imparted to me as well. I started to receive dreams and visions from the Holy Spirit and the power of Jesus transformed me into a possibility thinker. I'm now reaching my goals and living in my dreams. In fact, this book is the fruit of me being set free from impossibility thinking!

We Are in Christ

All praise to God, the Father of our Lord Jesus Christ, who has blessed us with every spiritual blessing in the heavenly realms because we are united with Christ. Even before he made the world, God loved us and chose us in Christ to be holy and without fault in his eyes. God decided in advance to adopt us into his own family by bringing us to himself through Jesus Christ. This is what he wanted to do, and it gave him great pleasure (Eph. 1:3-5 NLT).

You and I are never defined by either our family lines or a broken past. We have a new identity, because we have been grafted into the family tree of Jesus Christ. In Christ, we have received a new inheritance as His blessed children. Because of this, we have now inherited all spiritual blessings of heaven. We are the children of God *"And since we are his children, we are his heirs. In fact, together with Christ we are heirs of God's glory"* (Rom 8:17 NLT). The glory of God is our inheritance. We can enjoy full freedom from every generational curse. This happens when we get revelation of how we have died with Christ. The patterns of generational sins have been broken, and we can walk in our inheritance as His sons and daughters. This will affect the coming generations as well. They will not have to fight our battles. They will instead receive a big inheritance of generational blessings. This is very good news for all of us who have had to struggle to overcome our broken past. Our kids will not have to fight the same battles.

Passing on an Inheritance to Coming Generations

...blessing I will bless you, and multiplying I will multiply your descendants as the stars of the heaven and as the sand which is on the seashore; and your descendants shall possess the gate of their enemies. In your seed all the nations of the earth shall be blessed, because you have obeyed My voice (Gen. 22:17-18 NKJV).

How great are his signs, how mighty his wonders! His kingdom is an eternal kingdom; his dominion endures from generation to generation (Dan. 4:3 NIV).

Our Father's plan was never to just deliver us from the ungodly inheritance of the past generations. He wants us to live in all the blessings that we have received in Christ and the full inheritance of our sonship. The Father's plan is for the breakthroughs and all our victories to become an inheritance of generational blessings, that we pass on to our children and the coming generations. The Kingdom of God always operates with generations in mind. God wants our spiritual inheritance to be multiplied in the lives of our children, so that they can extend the kingdom of God even much further than we have been able to do in our lifetime. This is the most important reason why freedom from generational curses is such good news. Our breakthroughs affect coming generations in a very powerful way, and we need to have a vision for how to pass on a big inheritance of generational blessings to our children and children's children. Getting a revelation of the Father's love and being established in a lifestyle where His love flows through our lives, will never just affect our lives. It will touch the lives of coming generations in a powerful way as well.

Summary

The love of the Father transforms our whole being. As we abide in that love, the fruit will always be more Christlikeness. For such a long time, we have been led to believe that the key to personal restoration and sanctification is to be found in being disciplined. The truth is that we have never been able to change ourselves. It is only the love of the Father can do that. In this part of the book, we have been exploring how abiding in His love bring healing to our soul, as our mind, will and emotional lives are delivered and healed by the power of Christ. There is hope and healing for all of us through the love of the Father!

Activations

- We read 1 Pet. 1:18-19 and Gal. 3:13-14, in this chapter. Spend some time reflecting on these passages with the Holy Spirit. Invite Him to provide more insights from these passages, so that you can begin to live in the full freedom from generational curses that Jesus has given to you through the cross. Write down what He reveals to you.

- We read about how an ungodly inheritance has been passed through the generations of most families. Take some time in prayer, to ask the Father to reveal these generational curses in your family. Ask for revelation on the strongholds this inheritance has created in your life, as well as the godly strongholds of blessings that He wants to replace them with. Write down what He reveals to you.

- Take 20-30 minutes in prayer. Ask the Father to clean up your family tree from all generational sins. Break the generational curses in your life and ask the Father to replace the strongholds of these curses with godly strongholds of generational blessings.

- Spend some time with the Father and write a vision of the generational blessings that you want to pass on to your children and coming generations. Ask Him for a plan with concrete steps about how to create and pass on an inheritance of generational blessings. Write this plan down, together with the vision of the inheritance of generational blessings that you received from God. Begin to take steps to align with and fulfill this plan as soon as possible.

Part 3:

From Bondage to Freedom

In this part of the book, we are going to study some of the areas where we will experience a paradigm shift, as a fruit of learning to abide in the Father's love. Abiding in His love will transform us into the image of Christ. Sometimes, when we're teaching on Christlikeness and our freedom in Him, we do so in very general terms. But it's very important for us to know what our freedom in Christ really looks like, so that we can live with a clear vision of what we are growing into. In this part of the book, we will look at several areas, where we will be set free from bondage into full freedom, by the power of the Holy Spirit.

The reason I have picked these areas is because they are the ones where God has done powerful things in my life. My hope is that by reading the coming chapters, you will be encouraged to allow God to work within you in these areas as well.

CHAPTER 15: FROM THE HEAD TO THE HEART

"So above all, guard the affections of your heart, for they affect all that you are. Pay attention to the welfare of your innermost being, for from there flows the wellspring of life" (Prov. 4:23 TPT).

The heart is the center of man. The Greek word for heart is *kardia,* which also means center. We *have* emotions, the will, and mind. They are all part of the human soul, but our heart is something deeper than that. When the Word of God mentions our hearts, it speaks about the center of our entire being. The heart is the core of who we *are,* as human beings. It's because of this, that our God works with heart transformation, not by behavior modification. Religion lacks the power to transform our hearts and is therefore conditioned to work with behavior management. In contrast, the Father changes our behavior by transforming our hearts. He does this because once our hearts have been transformed, our lifestyle will change as well.

Man Has Lost the Ability to Live from the Heart

One of the unfortunate consequences of mankind's fall into sin is that we lost our ability to live from the heart. Humans have now instead been conditioned to live through trusting the mind. This means that the unregenerate, natural man, must trust in his own intellectual capacity to determine right from wrong or good from evil. This was the result of man eating from the tree of knowledge of good and evil (Gen. 3:6-7). Out of that tree has grown all the political systems, religions and philosophies, by which man tries to find identity, meaning, and define what is good and evil in the sight of God. Adam and Eve were invited to eat from the Tree of Life. If they had done that, they would have been filled with the life of God and they would have been able to live by His life.

Only by being filled with the life of God can we begin to live from the heart. By eating from the tree of knowledge of good and evil, the eyes of man were opened to know good and evil. When that happened, the eyes of their hearts were closed. The result of this was devastating, since mankind then lost their ability to relate to God. The Father had to find other ways to communicate with us, until the time when Jesus came and undid the damage of the fall.

Our Father Is a Heart-to-Heart God

By studying the Scriptures, it is easy to see how the Father wishes to relate to us by the heart. I often say that God is a heart-to-heart God. The Lord opens our heart, by inviting us to fellowship with Himself. When we live in intimacy with God, the Holy Spirit fills our heart with the love of the Father and a deep revelation of His Son (Rom. 5:5, Eph. 1:17-19). This is how our hearts are renewed, so that we can begin to live from the heart once again. We're now going to read some verses that reveal how vital it is for us to live from the heart:

- *Trust in the LORD with all thine heart; and lean not unto thine own understanding (Prov. 3:5).*

  We are encouraged to trust the Lord with all our heart and not to trust in our own capacity to figure out life by ourselves. This is because He is way smarter than we are. One of the New Covenant blessings is that Jesus Christ Himself has become our wisdom. We can trust in Him to lead and guide us every step of the way, and the wisdom of God can never be grasped intellectually. It comes by a revelation when the Holy Spirit enlightens our heart.

- *Keep your heart with all diligence, for out of it spring the issues of life (Prov. 4:23 NKJV).*

  The reason that it is so important to protect our hearts is

that the heart is the core of who we are. What we allow to shape our hearts, will sooner or later become our lives. All transformation begins by us surrendering our hearts to the Father. When we give Him our hearts, we will be healed and transformed by His love operating within us. As we keep on receiving from Him, the love of the Father becomes a shield that protects our hearts. We become so full of His love that sin, our false identities, and all other destructive things no longer finds a place in our hearts. This is what Jesus meant when He said that the devil had nothing in Him (John 14:30).

- *A new heart also will I give you, and a new spirit will I put within you: and I will take away the stony heart out of your flesh, and I will give you an heart of flesh. And I will put my spirit within you, and cause you to walk in my statutes, and ye shall keep my judgments, and do them (Ezek. 36:26-27).*

When we were born again, our hearts were cleansed and totally renewed. The believer has been filled with the life of God, so that the eyes of the heart can be opened once again. It was not that our old heart was totally removed and another was put in its place. We have received a new heart in the sense of it being cleansed, restored, and filled with the Father's love. Because of this, our spirits have come alive. We are now in a relationship with the Father, where we can relate to Him heart-to-heart.

- *Blessed are the pure in heart: for they shall see God (Matt. 5:8).*

Notice that Jesus didn't say that the pure in doctrine will see God, but the pure in heart. This is because God can't be grasped by the mind, but true revelation of who God is will always illuminate the heart first, which then leads to the renewing of the mind. A true revelation of Christ transforms our theology and doctrines as well. True faith is always built on revelation. All true knowledge about God comes to us in that way. Therefore, we need to keep our hearts open and honest before Him.

- *...and hope maketh not ashamed; because the love of God is shed abroad in our hearts by the Holy Ghost which is given unto us (Rom. 5:5).*

  The love of the Father has been poured into our heart by the Holy Spirit. Remember that the heart is our real core, so when the love of God is present and operating within our hearts, our lives are transformed by His love. A fruit of having His love in our hearts is that it becomes natural for us to love people as well. When we were born again, loving people became part of our new nature. Therefore, it is natural for us to love people and to live a lifestyle of Christlike self-giving love. It's no longer natural for us to carry disappointment, bitterness, or to live selfishly. We have the love of God within our heart, and loving people has become the natural thing for us to do.

- *... that the God of our Lord Jesus Christ, the Father of glory, may give you a spirit of wisdom and of revelation in the knowledge of Him. I pray that the eyes of your heart may be enlightened, so that you will know what is the hope of His calling, what are the riches of the glory of His inheritance in the saints, and what is the boundless greatness of His power toward us who believe (Eph. 1:17-19 NASB).*

  The Holy Spirit reveal the inheritance that we have been given as children of God, by enlightening the eyes of our hearts to the glorious realities of the New Covenant. The salvation we have received in Christ is so vastly glorious and rich, that we need the Holy Spirit to begin to grasp it even a little. An important part of our inheritance is to start to live in all the blessings that we have as sons and daughters. For us to do that, we need help because this new lifestyle is so contrary to our former way of life. That help is given to us as the Holy Spirit enlightens our heart by revelation.

- *For this is the covenant that I will make with the house of Israel after those days, saith the Lord; I will put my laws into their mind, and write them in their hearts (Hebr. 8:10, see also Hebr. 10:16).*

We gain access to the will of God for our lives, when our hearts are quickened by the Father's love. This is because the will of God has been written upon our hearts and it's revealed to us through our fellowship with Christ. When His wisdom enlightens our hearts, we will also perceive His will. The Father has chosen to reveal all His purposes in this way, so that the only way to live in His will is if we live in intimacy with Him. We cannot find the will of the Father by ourselves and neither can we do His will, if we don't learn to abide within His love. This is the key to true knowledge and wisdom. As His will is revealed to us, His grace will empower us to do whatever He asks of us. With every revelation we receive from Him comes a divine enablement so that we can live it out.

Jesus Is the Tree of Life

The thief comes only to steal and kill and destroy; I came so that they would have life, and have it abundantly (John 10:10 NASB).

For God so loved the world, that He gave His only Son, so that everyone who believes in Him will not perish, but have eternal life… The Father loves the Son and has entrusted all things to His hand. The one who believes in the Son has eternal life; but the one who does not obey the

Son will not see life, but the wrath of God remains on him (John 3:16, 35-36 NASB).

Jesus Himself is the tree of life and by receiving Him, we receive the life of God. Eternal life is called eternal, simply because it is the life of Christ. When we were born again, the life of God was imparted into us and we became children of God. He has always been our Father, in the sense that He is our Creator. Being born again means that God has now become our Father through birth as well. Because of this, we can now live by the indwelling life of Christ. It is by learning to live by His life of that we begin to live from our hearts. It is never possible to learn how to live from the heart by knowledge or principle alone. To truly begin to live with the Father from the heart, is built on us being in union with Him. When we learn to walk in intimate relationship with the Father, then our hearts will be opened more and more so that we will be able to experience more of His love for us.

Our Heart Is Quickened by the Love of God

The Holy Spirit fills our hearts with the love of God. This is an important part of His ministry as our Helper. *"And this hope will not lead to disappointment. For we know how dearly God loves us, because he has given us the Holy Spirit to fill our hearts with his love"* (Rom. 5:5 NLT). Sometimes, we might struggle when it comes to receiving the love of the Father. The good news for us who have found it difficult to receive from God, is that the Holy Spirit helps us to become good receivers. It is His job to open our heart and fill it with the love of God. This is a somewhat overlooked, but still very important part of His ministry. When we think of the baptism of the Holy Spirit, we usually think of these two verses:

"As for me, I baptize you with water; but He is coming who is mightier than I, and I am not fit to untie the straps of His sandals; He will baptize you with the Holy Spirit and fire" (Luke 3:16 NASB).

But ye shall receive power, after that the Holy Ghost is come upon you: and ye shall be witnesses unto me both in Jerusalem, and in all Judæa, and in Samaria, and unto the uttermost part of the earth (Acts 1:8).

These verses describe how the Holy Spirit wants to empower us to become witnesses by filling us with power. This is an awesome promise and to be flowing in the power of God is a big part of a victorious christian life. However, we must remember that all the manifestations of the power of God that we get to experience are always meant to be a demonstration of His great love. When we are filled with the Holy Spirit, He pours the Father's love into our hearts. The more we learn to receive and abide within the love of the Father, the more sensitive and open we will be to discern the voice of the Holy Spirit. The baptism of the Holy Spirit is always a baptism of love and it opens our hearts to receive from God.

We Can't Open Our Hearts, but He Can

Throughout my years in itinerant ministry, there is one question that people have kept asking, repeatedly. This has been the case wherever I've been traveling in the world. That simple question is: "How do I open my heart to receive His love?" The reality is that we can't do that by ourselves. It is only the Holy Spirit that can open a closed heart to the Father's love, but we can surrender our hearts to Him and make our life available for transformation. This is what Jesus wanted to accomplish by speaking in parables:

And the disciples came and said to Him, "Why do You speak to them in parables?" He answered and said to them, "Because it has been given to you to know the mysteries of the kingdom of heaven, but to them it has not been given. For whoever has, to him more will be given, and he will have abundance; but whoever does not have, even what he has will be taken away from him. Therefore I speak to them in parables, because seeing they do not see, and hearing they do not hear, nor do they

It would be a huge misunderstanding to think that Jesus spoke in parables to make His teachings more accessible for the people, or easier to understand. The real reason that Jesus was speaking in parables was to hide the mysteries of the Kingdom, so that the people had to come to Him to understand any of His teachings. The same is true today. Only by living in an intimate relationship with the Father, can we begin to understand the Bible the way in which He intended. When Jesus speaks about eyes that cannot see and ears that can't hear, He is obviously not talking about our physical eyes and ears. He is describing the eyes and ears of the heart. The people who heard Him speak, but couldn't receive His words, were unable to hear because their hearts were hardened. When the heart is hardened, we can't perceive the voice of Jesus and we are unable to discern the secrets of the Kingdom. This is because we can only perceive what the Father is doing or saying, through our spiritual senses. Consequently, the person whose heart has been hardened will not come to Jesus and find healing.

Jesus said that it was people with a hardened heart, that fulfilled the prophecy of Isaiah. This specific prophecy is also mentioned in other places in the New Testament. This reveal how important the human heart really is to the Father (John 12:37-40, Acts 28:25-28). What happened to the people that had responded to Jesus by surrendering their hearts to Him and had become His disciples? Their ears were opened to hear the voice of their Father and their spiritual eyes were opened to see the secrets of the Kingdom. As a result, they came to Jesus to find healing for their hearts.

The Surrendered Heart

When we surrender our heart to Jesus, He wants to fill our hearts with the love of the Father. It is when this love is poured into our heart, that the process of restoring our spiritual sight and hearing begins. We are unable to open our heart to receive from Him by ourselves, but we can surrender our hearts to Him. To make our hearts available to Him needs to be our daily choice and priority, where we give Jesus full access to do whatever He wants in our lives. All of this happens as a fruit of us abiding in the love of the Father. This was so important to Paul, that he even describes the mandate that he was given by Jesus, with these powerful words:

...delivering thee from the people, and from the Gentiles, unto whom now I send thee, to open their eyes, and to turn them from darkness to light, and from the power of Satan unto God, that they may receive forgiveness of sins, and inheritance among them which are sanctified by faith that is in me (Acts 26:17-18).

Jesus spoke of His mission as one of opening the eyes of the blind as well (Luke 4:18). We have already seen earlier in this chapter, that this is the ministry of the Spirit as well (Eph. 1:17-18). Seeing with the eyes of the heart, enabled Jesus to see and do the works of the Father (John 5:19).

From Intellectual to Relational Christianity

Learning to live from the heart means that we quit trying to make sense of our lives with God through reasoning alone. Because it's totally impossible for us to understand the Father by ourselves, being delivered from the burden of trying to figure Him out is a very big relief. There is a big difference between living with God at a distance, where we are left alone to find His will, compared to living in an intimate relationship with our heavenly Father, in which He reveals Himself to us. The former is very man-centered and legalistic, while living with the Father places all the focus on Him. This is the glorious freedom that we have been called into. As our hearts are opened to His love, we're learning to live out of our heart-to-heart relationship with the Father. The important thing for us will be to abide in His love. When we learn to live in that place, our relationship with God will be our treasure. As we learn to live from the heart we're fulfilling the will of God, doing the works that the Father is showing us.

Seeing with the Eyes of the Heart

I have often been asked about strategies and visions. Specifically, people have wanted to know how I've been able to fulfill the call upon my life and my prophetic words. The truth is that I am not good with formulating visions or strategies. The way that I have learned to partner with the Father, is to simply do what I see Him doing. In the process of walking that out, I then begin to put into words what He has written on my heart. This is how I formulate my vision. This usually turns out to be very strategic, because as I live in His timing, new doors for ministry will always open and that helps me to reach more people. The Father knows best what to do, even if it sometimes comes as a surprise to me. This doesn't mean that I have no long-term visions or plans. In fact, I do have many long-term plans. The leading of the Holy Spirit isn't always spontaneous and in the moment. Sometimes, He will lead us by giving us a word that will take years, or even a lifetime to fulfill. Our callings will look different, but living in intimacy with the Father always gives us big visions, because He loves to co-labor with us.

Condemnation Closes the Heart

One thing that will block our spiritual sight and hearing quickly, is the power of religious guilt and condemnation. This is because religion doesn't operate by the life of Jesus, but by the knowledge of good and evil. John wrote:

We will know by this that we are of the truth, and will set our heart at ease before Him, that if our heart condemns us, that God is greater than our heart, and He knows all things. Beloved, if our heart does not condemn us, we have confidence before God (1 John 3:19-21 NASB).

When we come under religious influence and oppression, we can no longer relate to God from the heart. Religion will condition us to trust our reasoning again. That will cause our hearts to harden. This is the reason why it is so important to protect our heart from legalism. When I got saved, I heard a lot of teaching on protecting the heart. This was a good and biblical teaching. My problem was that I didn't know how to apply it very well, but over time I have discovered that the best way to protect my heart is by abiding in the Father's love. I have realized that my heart will be protected, as I stay focused on the one thing that can keep my heart pure — the love of the Father.

Loving God with Our Mind

Our minds and intellect are wonderful gifts from the Father, and knowledge and theological studies can often be valuable. I have deeply enjoyed my theological studies and I have grown a lot in my relationship with the Father through all these studies. We are called to love God with everything that we are. This includes our mind and thoughts as well. *"You shall love the Lord your God with all your heart, and with all your soul, and with all your mind.' This is the great and foremost commandment. The second is like it, 'You shall love your neighbor as yourself"* (Matt. 22:37-39 NASB). To study and think about the Kingdom of God can be very valuable, especially when done in the context of a life built on intimacy with Christ. This is one of the ways, through which the Holy Spirit enlightens our heart. The point of this chapter isn't that our intellect and the mind is worthless. Rather, it is that we can't build our life with God by trusting in our own intellect and reasoning. The mind is good when we use it for the purpose that the Father gave it, but we were never meant to build our relationship with God through our intellectual understanding. A deep and intimate relationship with God can only develop when we learn to live from the heart.

Activations

- We read Prov. 4:23 and Rom. 5:5 in this chapter. Spend some time reflecting on these passages with the Holy Spirit. Invite Him to provide more insights from these passages so that you can begin to live from the heart, in an intimate relationship with your heavenly Father. Write down what He reveals to you.

- We saw how we have emotions, a will, and the mind. These are part of our soul, but our heart is the core of our being. It is who we are. Therefore, the Father work with heart transformation. What does this mean? Spend some time to reflect on this. Invite the Father to give more revelation on this topic and write down the insights you receive.

- Within this chapter there is a list of verses on the topic of the heart. Go back and read that list, while inviting the Holy Spirit to highlight one or two of these verses for you. Pray and meditate over these verses and ask the Holy Spirit to bring forth revelations from them. Write down what He reveals to you.

- Take 20-30 minutes in prayer. Ask the Father to pour His love into your heart. Take time to soak in His love and allow Him to baptize your heart in it. Make this a lifestyle and keep on doing this every day. When you do that, your heart will be constantly connected to His heart and love.

CHAPTER 16: GRACE IN WEAKNESS

Therefore, in order to keep me from becoming conceited, I was given a thorn in my flesh, a messenger of Satan, to torment me. Three times I pleaded with the Lord to take it away from me. But he said to me, "My grace is sufficient for you, for my power is made perfect in weakness. "Therefore I will boast all the more gladly about my weaknesses, so that Christ's power may rest on me (2 Cor. 12:7-9 NIV).

When looking at the verses above, we could probably get lost in speculations about what Paul really had in mind, when he spoke about the thorn in his flesh. Many people have tried to figure out what he meant, but we can't know for sure. I think that the most likely explanation is that his thorn in the flesh, was the man who oversaw the Jewish persecution against Paul. What we do know for sure is that this thorn was something that was uncomfortable for Paul and that it made him feel his weakness. It caused him to feel like he was out of control. All of us can relate to that on some level. We all have certain areas of our lives, where we struggle in a way that makes us feel both vulnerable and weak. This struggle might be related to a difficult relationship, a situation at work, or a struggle with a certain sin that we are unable to overcome. The way of the flesh is to find strategies to get rid of our weaknesses, by becoming stronger and taking control of our lives. No one like to feel weak and there is a temptation for us to find ways to try to overcome in our own strength. The gospel shows us a different way, by leading us to give up control and trust in His grace.

His Strength in Our Weaknesses

When Paul asked the Father to remove the thorn in his flesh, he didn't receive the answer that he wanted. He prayed three times, but the thorn didn't leave. God gave him a different answer than he had expected. He told Paul: *"My grace is sufficient for thee, for my strength is made perfect in weakness"*. There is a powerful truth hidden in this answer. We learn that Paul prayed multiple times to be delivered from this thorn, that had caused him to feel weak. I believe most of us can relate to that. When we are reminded of our weaknesses, we want to get out of these situations that reveal our pain as soon as possible. It doesn't feel good to be weak.

Sometimes, I have even talked to people who believe that if we're really walking by faith, we will never face pain or weakness. That is not true. Just like Paul had to face his thorn in the flesh, we will also have to deal with our weaknesses. Our Father has a specific goal in mind when allowing this to happen, which is to deliver us from trusting in our own strength, so that we can learn to trust in His grace instead. This is the reason we often receive a similar answer to the one that Paul received. Our Father will usually not remove the things in our lives that expose our weakness. Instead, He will let the weak places in our lives become portals, through which He expresses His power and love. The Passion translation words the passage that we just read like this:

But he answered me, "My grace is always more than enough for you, and my power finds its full expression through your weakness." So I will celebrate my weaknesses, for when I'm weak I sense more deeply the mighty power of Christ living in me. So I'm not defeated by my weakness, but delighted! For when I feel my weakness and endure mistreatment—when I'm surrounded with troubles on every side and face persecution because of my love for Christ—I am made yet stronger. For my weakness becomes a portal to God's power (2 Cor. 12:9-10 TPT)

Paul - A Weak Leader?

The culture which permeated Corinth was one where strength, a charismatic personality and being a good speaker were signs of good leadership. This is very much in line with how the culture of the western world views a good leader today. This culture had started to influence the church in Corinth, even to the point that Paul's apostolic ministry was heavily questioned and some even openly rejected him. He didn't live up to their expectation of the strong leader. When Paul wrote his second letter to them, He did it to defend the validity of his apostolic ministry. Here are some of the reasons why the people in Corinth believed that Paul was a weak leader:

- They found Paul to be a weak personality, who was not the dynamic leader they expected him to be, while at the same time he spoke with authority through his letters (1 Cor.10:1, 10-11)
- They were unimpressed by his looks and appearance (2 Cor. 10:10)
- They thought that his preaching amounted to nothing (2 Cor. 10:10-11)
- They accused him of lacking training in public speaking (2 Cor. 11:5)
- They confused Paul's kindness for lack of authority, and did not think he was as powerful as some of the so called "super apostles", in the church (2 Cor. 10:12, 11:5-15)

They thought like this because they were confusing our human strength with being strong in the spirit. They believed that Paul didn't act like a strong apostolic leader should do. The reason for that was that they had a very worldly definition of what a leader should look like and behave. Paul found his strength in the grace of God. Being strong in Christ looks very different, compared to our human strength. The grace of God can only be reached when we embrace our weaknesses with humility. This is why we need to be cleansed from our tendencies to operate in human strength if we want to live by the power of God.

Secure in His Identity

Paul wrote these words concerning his ministry: *"Even if I should choose to boast, I would not be a fool, because I would be speaking the truth. But I refrain, so no one will think more of me than is warranted by what I do or say, or because of these surpassingly great revelations"* (2 Cor. 12:6-7 NIV). This reveals to us how secure Paul was in his identity in Christ. The truth was that Paul had a lot to boast about and that he could have written many letters, just to talk about all his spiritual accomplishments. He could very easily have built a reputation and image with the Corinthian believers in this way. Since He knew that Christ is enough for us, he didn't want to do that. It takes courage and security in our identity in Christ to dare to live like that. This way of life was what made Paul appear very weak to the Corinthians. But to live like in true transparency will create an internal res and peace, because when we have dropped all our masks and appearances, we no longer need to protect our image. Then we can fully be resting in the Father's love, knowing that everything that He has given by grace, will be protected by His favor. It's totally fine to live with the appearance of weakness when we know that Christ is our strength.

The Ministry of Paul

In his first letter to the church in Corinth, Paul is giving an honest description of his ministry as an apostle of Jesus Christ. What he describes is a lifestyle of striking simplicity, where he often faced his own weaknesses and limitations. It was a lifestyle where the grace of God was on full display:

It seems to me that God has put us who bear his Message on stage in a theater in which no one wants to buy a ticket. We're something everyone stands around and stares at, like an accident in the street. We're the Messiah's misfits. You might be sure of yourselves, but we live in the midst of frailties and uncertainties. You might be well-

thought-of by others, but we're mostly kicked around. Much of the time we don't have enough to eat, we wear patched and threadbare clothes, we get doors slammed in our faces, and we pick up odd jobs anywhere we can to eke out a living. When they call us names, we say, "God bless you." When they spread rumors about us, we put in a good word for them. We're treated like garbage, the leftovers that nobody wants. And it's not getting any better (1 Cor. 4:9-13 The Message).

Paul had to daily choose a lifestyle where he was misunderstood, rejected and didn't have a lot of money. He was both slandered and persecuted, but he had learned to trust the grace of God to give him favor and open doors for his ministry. Because he knew the Father so well, he received all encouragement and comfort he needed from Him. That gave Paul strength to fulfill his calling (2 Cor. 1:3-6). God is not trying to make our lives as comfortable as possible by removing every weakness from our lives, so that we can serve Him. He wants to make us comfortable with our life by teaching us to trust His grace in our weakness, so that the power of Christ can rest upon us. In that way, our weakness becomes a portal for His power.

Areas of Weakness in Our Lives

The areas of our life where we feel the most weak and vulnerable, are the areas where the grace of God will manifest the strongest and in the most powerful way. As we have seen in this chapter, our weaknesses are meant to be portals to God's power. He longs to reveal His strength on our behalf. To accept this truth and live accordingly will take a lot of courage, but only when we learn to be vulnerable with our weakness, can we fully surrender it to the Father. Paul is describing what this lifestyle looks like here:

But we have this treasure in earthen vessels, that the excellence of the power may be of God and not of us. We are hard-pressed on every side, yet not crushed; we are perplexed, but not in despair; persecuted, but not forsaken; struck down, but not destroyed— always carrying about in the body the dying of the Lord Jesus, that the life of Jesus also may be manifested in our body. For we who live are always delivered to death for Jesus' sake, that the life of Jesus also may be manifested in our mortal flesh (2 Cor. 4:7-11 NKJV).

A life full of the power of Christ isn't a kind of life where we will no longer be exposed to human weakness. Rather it's a life where we learn to live within the tension between our human weakness and the resurrection life of Jesus. The Father will always meet us right there in our weaknesses, ready to display His power for us. Therefore, acknowledging and surrendering our weakness to the Father provides many wonderful opportunities to go deeper into our relationship with Him. It also teaches us to grow in humility and transparency, both before Christ and other people. Here are some areas that can reveal our human weaknesses:

- ***Human limitations***
  Human limitations could be things like a lack of strength because of age, finding it hard to handle all the demands at work, challenges in our families, or sometimes to just admit that there are certain things that we aren't good at or gifted to do. God gives grace to the humble and it's a huge sign of humility to realize that we are not good at everything, but that we need other people (1 Pet. 5:5-7). Understanding this will liberate us and make us way more effective in ministry, because then we can ask both God and other people for help. But to come to that place, we must admit our limitations and dare to be vulnerable and weak before God. When we do that, He will always provide an abundance of grace. So, when we surrender our limitations to God, the limitless power of Christ will rest upon us and work on our behalf.

- *Wounds and brokenness from the past*

   Another area that sometimes reveals our weaknesses are the painful memories, and the wounds of a broken past. Because of a very dark season in my past, I used to suffer from post-traumatic stress, which caused me problems to sleep and I had a lot of stress and anxiety in my heart. I asked the Father several times to deliver me from pain, but it took a couple of years to work through this pain to find healing. During that time, I learned a lot about being authentic and open, both before Jesus and other people. The help that I received through prayer and professional counseling, led me to a slow but steady recovery. It took time, but it was more than worth it. I learned that healing will eventually happen, if we dare to be transparent and open before the Father with all our pains. That gives Him the opportunity to shower us with His deep, comforting love. Being authentic and honest with Him is always the place where healing begin.

- *Sins that we can't overcome*

   As believers, we know that we shouldn't be struggling with sins, but sometimes we still do. For someone who loves God and wants to live with Christ, it can be deeply humiliating to come to terms with the fact that there are certain sins and habits that we can't overcome. All of us will struggle with habitual sins that seems to overpower us at times, and it becomes even more frustrating when we ask God to be delivered from them and nothing seem to change. I have talked to countless Christians that have struggled for years with certain sin that they cannot stop doing. They have tried everything, hoping to break free. They have talked to friends about it, received prayer and different kinds counseling, but they're still bound by the same issues. Struggling with bondages that we're unable to break free from reveals our weaknesses, almost more than anything else. One of the reasons why our way out of bondage takes time, might be that this is a very good way for us to learn to trust His grace. We need to be set free from trusting in our own ability to live for God, until there is nothing left for us, except Jesus Himself. This is sometimes a painful lesson, but the fruit of learning it is good. We learn both humility and patience in that way. When we stop trying to fix our lives and trust the grace of Christ, His power can work in us stronger than before.

God Gives Grace to The Humble

It takes a measure of humility to admit weaknesses, but since it's the humble who gains access to the grace of God, being open and honest about our weaknesses is the pathway to strength in God. *"But he giveth more grace. Wherefore he saith, God resisteth the proud, but giveth grace unto the humble"* (Jam. 4:7). The grace of God is His power operating, both in and through us. Spiritual strength has nothing to do with becoming stronger in ourselves. Rather it has to do with trusting in His strength. God is not trying to make us strong enough, so that He can use us. The Father wants to make us weak enough, so that we give up on our own strength. This gives Him space to work, both within and through us. This was how Paul could overcome His weakness: *"But by the grace of God I am what I am: and his grace which was bestowed upon me was not in vain; but I laboured more abundantly than they all: yet not I, but the grace of God which was with me"* (1 Cor. 15:10). Paul learned to trust the grace of God that was with him. By doing that he saw that in his human weakness, the power of Jesus Christ could operate in the most powerful way. Therefore, Paul even described the weak areas in his life as portal for God's power. This has been my own experience in my life with the Father as well. Most of my spiritual growth has happened because of me being humbled by my sins, failures, and weaknesses. The good news is that God gives grace to the humble

The Freedom of Being Weak

For years, I tried to become a stronger, holier and better believer. That became the religious mission of my life. Looking back, I can still remember the stress and pressure that this created in me. My heart was good and my motives were right. I even had a zeal for God, but because I lacked revelation of my identity in Christ and the Father's love, my relationship with God, became my personal project of self-improvement. It is very exhausting to live like that because the flesh is never satisfied with less than the unattainable goal of perfection. No matter how hard I tried, there was always more to be done. If I prayed one hour, I thought that I probably should have prayed two hours instead. When I finally overcame a certain sin, I realized that there were still many areas in my life where I struggled. I tried desperately to get rid of all weaknesses and become a strong believer. This ended in a spiritual burnout, which brought me to a place where I had to face my weaknesses and shortcomings. The good news is that I also met the grace of God! Since then, I've been on a journey in the opposite direction, one of giving up all my ambitions of becoming a strong believer altogether. I learned that in the kingdom of God, we grow up by growing down and we win by giving up. The strength of God is made perfect in our weakness. There waits for us a rest in Christ, that we enter, not by trying harder, but by giving up and trusting in Him. This is the glorious freedom of being a child of God!

Activations

- We studied 2 Cor. 12:6-10 in this chapter. Spend some time reflecting on these passages with the Holy Spirit. Invite Him to provide even more revelation from this passage, so that you can grow in a lifestyle where His grace is made perfect in your weaknesses. Write down what He reveals to you.

- We saw how our weaknesses becomes a portal for the power of Jesus. How does this work? Why is it easier for Him to use your weakness than your strength? Spend some time to reflect upon these questions. Then invite the Holy Spirit to give further revelation to you, on this topic. Write down what He reveals to you.

- Within this chapter, I wrote about three areas in which our weaknesses are often revealed. These three areas are:

    1. *Human limitations.*
    2. *Wounds and brokenness from the past.*
    3. *Sins that we can't overcome.*

Have you come to terms with your weaknesses within these areas? How does it feel to be weak? How do you handle them? Invite the Holy Spirit to speak to your heart in this area.

- Take 20-30 minutes in prayer. Ask the Father to make your weaknesses portals for His grace and the power of Christ. Ask Him to make you weak enough to really be moldable in His hands, so that His love can flow in and through your life freely.

CHAPTER 17: THE LOVE OF GOD CASTS OUT FEAR

The love of God is a powerful antidote to fear. Fear and love can't coexist, so when the Father's love is poured into our fearful heart, all fear will be cast out. *"Herein is our love made perfect, that we may have boldness in the day of judgment: because as he is, so are we in this world. There is no fear in love; but perfect love casteth out fear: because fear hath torment. He that feareth is not made perfect in love. We love him, because he first loved us"* (1 John 4:17-19). The only reason for a child of God to struggle with fear is that we haven't yet been made perfect in love. Whenever we discover that there is an area of fear in our hearts, we should view it as an invitation for us to grow in love.

I have struggled a lot with fear in my life. Earlier in my christian life, I always tried to fight against it. That didn't help me, because fear always grows if we focus on it. The more I tried to rebuke or pray against the fears in my life, the bigger they became. As I got a deeper revelation of the Father's love, I found out that a better way to for me to face my fears, was to simply acknowledge them to my Father, by asking Him to love me in those areas where fear had a hold on me. Once I learned to do that, His love started to flow into these areas of my heart and fear had to leave. Of course, this didn't happen instantly. Instead, getting delivered from all my fears happened through a process that took a couple of years. In fact, I'm still going through that process today because I am still being perfected in His love. But I have come a long way since I started. For that I'm very thankful!

Fear Is a Spiritual Weapon

Fear is one of the devil's most effective weapons, when it comes to keeping people in bondage. *"Forasmuch then as the children are partakers of flesh and blood, he also himself likewise took part of the same; that through death he might destroy him that had the power of death, that is, the devil; and deliver them who through fear of death were all their lifetime subject to bondage"* (Hebr. 2:14-15). Satan uses the fear of death to bind people. The fear of death is at the root of all other fears, since all our fears ultimately comes from being afraid of being harmed, or losing from something that is valuable. Jesus has now delivered us from the power of the fear of death so that we no longer need to be afraid of being harmed. This happened when we were crucified with Christ and lost our lives to gain His life instead (Gal. 2:19-21). We are now made alive in Christ and the Father's love is much stronger than even our worst fears!

For this reason, we now have a way out of all fear. Fear is a spirit and every spiritual power that opposes the Kingdom of God, has been defeated through the cross of Christ. We have been set free from the spirit of fear. The Father has now given us another spirit instead: *"For ye have not received the spirit of bondage again to fear; but ye have received the Spirit of adoption, whereby we cry, Abba, Father"* (Rom. 8:15). We used to be bound by the spirit of fear, but now we have received the Spirit of sonship, through which we're being liberated by God to walk in holy boldness, that comes from abiding in His love. We might still struggle with fear sometimes, but we are no longer powerless against it. If we have surrendered our lives to Christ, fear doesn't have any power over us, because the love of God is much stronger. When we walk in fear, it limits our life with the Father in several ways. The Bible even describes the fear of man as a snare.

The Fear of Man - a Snare

It is rather obvious that walking in the fear of man, will limit us dramatically in a lot of ways. *"The fear of man brings a snare, but whoever trusts in the Lord shall be safe"* (Prov. 29:25 NKJV). Walking in the fear of man snares us from being able to live in the glorious freedom of our sonship. There will come times when the Father leads us to take steps, or make decisions, that will be unpopular and make us look foolish in the eyes of other people. It is a huge temptation for all of us to give in to the opinions and attitudes of other people, just to keep the peace and save our reputation. But that type of peace is false peace, which it is not built on the truth. In Scandinavia, balance and diplomacy are very important parts of our culture, but heavenly balance looks extremely different to how Scandinavian, or our Swedish culture define them.

I love Scandinavia and I'm grateful for a lot of things within our culture, but there have been times when God has called me to do things that isn't in line with our way of life. To do what God has led me to do in some of these situations, I have had to overcome the fear of rejection. As the fear of man starts to rise in my heart, I have learned to stop what I'm doing and spend some time with the Father. I focus on His heart by actively receiving His love and that gives me strength to do what God calls me to do, even if I'm afraid at times. The Father's love sets me free to make the right decision even when it is a challenging one. It's very encouraging to think about the freedom that we find when the fear of man has been overcome in our lives. People can't control us if we are free from fear of their reactions and opinions.

Fear Quenches the Gifts of the Spirit

"Wherefore I put thee in remembrance that thou stir up the gift of God, which is in thee by the putting on of my hands. For God hath not given us the spirit of fear; but of power, and of love, and of a sound mind" (2 Tim. 1:6-7).

Another consequence of walking in fear, is that it quenches the flow of the gifts of the Spirit. It's very hard to serve people in love and freedom, if we fear what they might think of us. Walking in the love and freedom of Christ is necessary, if we want the gifts of the Holy Spirit to operate through us. The good news is that the Holy Spirit isn't passive when His gifts have been quenched within our lives.

He provides strength and love to us, so that our gift can be stirred up. As the Holy Spirit pours the love of God into our hearts and we take steps of faith to minister to people, the gifts of the Spirit will be stirred up and revived within us. The problem is that fear makes us passive. It is very hard to connect with the flow of the Holy Spirit when we're staying passive. I have learned to be very intentional in this area. When something happens that make me discouraged and feelings of hopelessness starts sneaking up on me, I take active steps to minister to someone. Maybe I'll pray for a person in need of healing, or I might find someone in need of a prophetic word. There will always be people present, in need of our prayer or encouragement. Ministering to these people might be as simple as sending an encouraging text message. I do this, because I know that as soon as I take a step to serve other people, the anointing and the fire of God is stirred up in me once again.

What About the Fear of God?

One of the questions people ask when they hear me teach on how the love of the Father casts out all fears, is how this relates to the fear of God. This is a valid question. We find many verses within the Bible, that speaks strongly about this. Here is one example: *"And I say unto you my friends, be not afraid of them that kill the body, and after that have no more that they can do. But I will forewarn you whom ye shall fear: Fear him, which after he hath killed hath power to cast into hell; yea, I say unto you, Fear him" (Luke 12:4-5).* Here, Jesus is speaking about the fear of God in a very strong language. Both the Psalms and the book of Proverbs, declare that the fear of God is the beginning of wisdom (Ps. 111:10, Prov. 1:7, 9:10).

This means that to live in the fear of God is foundational for us if we want to be wise. The problem is that many people confuse the fear of God with fear of punishment. We saw earlier that there is no fear in love. The Father's love casts out the type of fear that is connected to punishment. The fear of punishment means that a person is afraid of what God will do with us, if we fail to do what He has commanded us to do, but that is not the fear of God. This is the fear of what God threatens to do with us if we fail to obey Him. This creates a very controlling and authoritarian picture of God, which is the reason why some people never want to speak about the fear of God at all.

It's impossible to build healthy relationships based on the fear of punishment. For example, I could try to raise my kids by threats of punishment and I could even make them obey by doing that. However, as they grow up this will not work anymore and they will probably want to leave our home and move out as soon as possible. They would be right in doing so, since their upbringing wasn't built on love or respect. In other words, they didn't obey because we had a mutual respect, but because they were afraid of what I would do to them if they failed. That is not a good way to build healthy relationships, not with our families and neither with our Father. This isn't at all what the fear of God is about. In His confrontation with Satan, Jesus reveals what it means to fear God. True fear of God goes very well together with knowing God as our Father.

The Fear of God Equals Worship

When Jesus was tempted by the devil in the wilderness, one of the temptations involves Satan offering to give Jesus the nations with all their glory. This is what happened:

Next the devil took him to the peak of a very high mountain and showed him all the kingdoms of the world and their glory. "I will give it all to you," he said, "if you will kneel down and worship me." Get out of here, Satan," Jesus told him. "For the Scriptures say, 'You must worship the Lord your God and serve only him.' " Then the devil went away, and angels came and took care of Jesus. (Matt. 4:8-11 NLT).

This was not a trick question. Adam had committed high treason against God and handed the rule over this world over to Satan. Because of this, Satan had real power to give the nations to Jesus. Satan is called the god of this world and he was its rightful ruler (2 Cor. 4:4). Jesus knew this, but He knew even more that He was sent here to destroy the works of the devil (1 John 3:8). Jesus was never fooled by the devil's temptation, because He knew that this was going to happen through the cross, not by Him grabbing for worldly power. Jesus overcame this temptation by quoting this scripture from Deuteronomy: *"Thou shalt fear the LORD thy God, and serve him" (Deut. 6:13).*

When Jesus quoted this verse in the wilderness, He replaced the word *"fear"* with *"worship"*. This means that Jesus describes the fear of God as worship. In other words, to fear the Lord is to be captivated by His beauty and to be in awe of who He is. To walk in the fear of God equals a lifestyle of worship. This has nothing to do with the fear of punishment but it has everything to do with respect for the glory of God and His character, which means that the more we grow in revelation of the Father's love and the more that the glory of Jesus Christ is unveiled to us, the more we will be established in the fear of God. The love of the Father and the fear of God matches perfectly together, since both flows from the revelation of His heart. The more we get to know Him, the more our hearts will be filled with worship and reverence for Him.

Freedom from Fear Is Our Inheritance

As we are being established in the Father's love, we find freedom from all fear, so that we can live boldly with God. We are to make our progress in such a visible and obvious way, that our lives can become an inspiration for people that watch us. This is how Paul encouraged Timothy to live:

Don't let anyone think less of you because you are young. Be an example to all believers in what you say, in the way you live, in your love, your faith, and your purity. Until I get there, focus on reading the Scriptures to the church, encouraging the believers, and teaching them. Do not neglect the spiritual gift you received through the prophecy spoken over you when the elders of the church laid their hands on you. Give your complete attention to these matters. Throw yourself into your tasks so that everyone will see your progress. Keep a close watch on how you live and on your teaching. Stay true to what is right for the sake of your own salvation and the salvation of those who hear you (1 Tim. 4:12-16 NLT).

Paul instructed Timothy not to give in to people's opinion about him, or to allow them to put him down because he was a young leader. Instead, Paul tells Timothy to be an example in and to be a good teacher. Paul told Timothy to not neglect his spiritual gifts and to make sure that everyone could see his growth in the love of God. Why? Because that sets an example for other believers to follow! We need to make it our goal to live in such a way that the people who we meet can observe how we're growing in the love of the Father. We will open the door for them to come with us on a journey into the deeper things of God. We need to realize that our breakthroughs, are never just about us. It usually starts with God working in our lives, but as we are transformed, God wants our victories to be multiplied in other people. Timothy is a very good example of this. In the next chapter, we will look at his life to gain some more insights into this.

- We studied 1 John. 4:17-19 in this chapter. Spend some time reflecting on these passages with the Holy Spirit. Invite Him to provide even more revelation from this passage, so that you can grow in the revelation of how His love casts out all your fears. Write down what He reveals to you.

- We saw how the fear of man brings a snare for our life (Prov 29:25). What does this mean? Have you been in a situation where you struggled with fear of man? Did you overcome or give in to it? Spend time to reflect on these questions. Invite the Holy Spirit to speak to you. Write down the insights you find.

- Take 20-30 minutes in prayer. Invite the Holy Spirit to replace fear with love, power, and a sound mind. We saw that this is what the Holy Spirit gives to us (2 Tim. 1:6-7). Ask him to baptize your heart in the love of the Father, to strengthen you with wisdom and to fill you with His power, so that you become even bolder.

- In this chapter, we discovered the difference between the fear of God and the fear of punishment. Since the fear of God equals a worshipping lifestyle, ask Him to make you a worshiper. Our Father is so good that it is scary! Ask Him to reveal more of His beauty to you. Spend time to worship Him in spirit and truth.

CHAPTER 18: TIMOTHY - DELIVERED FROM FEAR

Most of us have probably already heard about Timothy. Since we love to read and study the Bible, we know that Paul mentions his name quite often. So, who was Timothy and why is he important to us? The name Timothy, or literally Timotheus, means *"dear to God"*. He was the son of a believing Jewish woman, whose name was Eunice. His father was a Greek man. This is how Timothy's story began:

Paul went first to Derbe and then to Lystra, where there was a young disciple named Timothy. His mother was a Jewish believer, but his father was a Greek. Timothy was well thought of by the believers in Lystra and Iconium, so Paul wanted him to join them on their journey. In deference to the Jews of the area, he arranged for Timothy to be circumcised before they left, for everyone knew that his father was a Greek (Acts 16:1-3 NLT).

Timothy- a Man Who Reaped Generational Blessings

Both Timothy's mother and grandmother are described as being women of strong faith. Timothy was born into a family, in which he had received a lot of generational blessings through their rich spiritual inheritance (2 Tim. 1:5). Sometimes, when people hear a testimony like mine, they almost wish that they had come from a more broken background, so that they could have a powerful salvation experience as well. That is a very flawed way to think. A way more powerful testimony is to have been raised within a line of generational blessings, and to be kept by the Father's love from childhood. It is an amazing honor to reap the generational blessings from our parents and we should be very grateful, if that is our family inheritance. The father of Timothy was a Greek man and he grew up and lived in the Lycaonian city of Lystra, in Asia Minor before he joined Paul's team (Acts 16:1-2).

Timothy Joins Paul

Paul met Timothy in Lystra, when he returned to visit the church that He and Barnabas had planted on their previous mission trip. He decided to bring Timothy with him as his co-worker which is why they circumcised him. Timothy became almost like a son to Paul and he grew into his closest and most trusted partner (Phil. 2:19-22). We get some insights into their relationship through the first and second letter to Timothy. These letters are fascinating to read, because they are personal letters from Paul to Timothy. In several of his other letters, Paul also mentions Timothy as the co-author of them. These are the letters that Timothy co-authored:

- 2 Corinthians (2 Cor. 1:1).
- Philippians (Phil. 1:1).
- Colossians (Col. 1:1).
- 1 Thessalonians (1 Thess. 1:1).
- 2 Thessalonians (2 Thess. 1:1).
- Philemon (Philemon 1).

As we have already seen, spiritual growth and the fulfillment of our calling are both very much affected by the type of people that we're allowing to influence us the most. We all need mentors that can help us, by holding us accountable to live in the full potential that the Father has put into our hearts (Read my book, *Partnering with the Love of Christ*, for more on this topic).

The Character of Timothy

But I trust in the Lord Jesus to send Timotheus shortly unto you, that I also may be of good comfort, when I know your state. For I have no man likeminded, who will naturally care for your state. For all seek their own, not the things which are Jesus Christ's. But ye know the proof of him, that, as a son with the father, he hath served with me in the gospel. Him therefore I hope to send presently, so soon as I shall see how it will go with me (Phil. 2:19-23).

There are some important character traits of Timothy, that really stands out when we're studying his life and ministry. His home church held him in very high regard. He was also a humble man and a very a good team member who got along well with others. This made him a highly appreciated member among Paul's team. By even being willing to be circumcised to reach people with the gospel, Timothy showed his adaptability and love for the people (Acts 16:2-3). Timothy's mother was a Jewish woman of a sincere faith, but since he had been raised in a culture that was shaped much more by the Greek mindset and lifestyle being circumcised probably wasn't what he wanted. For him to be willing to do that shows us that he was willing to make great personal sacrifices to reach people with the gospel.

The way that Paul trusted Timothy by sending him on important trips as his representative several times, reveal that Timothy was a caring and faithful man (1 Cor. 4:17, 16:10, Phil. 2:19). Knowing how much the churches meant to Paul, we can safely assume that when he sent someone to minister to them in his place, Paul only picked his most trusted friends. Paul wrote these words to the Corinthians: *"For this cause have I sent unto you Timotheus, who is my beloved son, and faithful in the Lord, who shall bring you into remembrance of my ways which be in Christ, as I teach every where in every church (1 Cor. 4:17).* Paul knew that Timothy would do what needed to be done, representing Paul in the best way possible by caring deeply for the people and churches to which he had been sent to minister. This reveals much about the kind of man that Timothy was. Both being able to make personal sacrifices and to stay faithful to our friends, are vital parts of being part of a good and dynamic team. We can be very gifted, but that doesn't make us easier to work with. Gifting without humility usually leads to arrogance. But humility causes us to be faithful and adaptable so that we can co-labor with others in fruitful ways.

The Weaknesses of Timothy

Now if Timotheus come, see that he may be with you without fear: for he worketh the work of the Lord, as I also do. Let no man therefore despise him: but conduct him forth in peace, that he may come unto me: for I look for him with the brethren (1 Cor. 16:10-11).

I'm writing to encourage you to fan into a flame and rekindle the fire of the spiritual gift God imparted to you when I laid my hands upon you. For God will never give you the spirit of fear, but the Holy Spirit who gives you mighty power, love, and self-control. So never be ashamed of the testimony of our Lord, nor be embarrassed over my imprisonment, but overcome every evil by the revelation of the power of God (2 Tim. 1:6-8 TPT)!

As a leader, it seems like Timothy struggled with some fear. This issue caused him to allow people to look down on him and walk over him. It's one thing that some people don't see our true value or that they decide to disrespect us. That is of course their choice, but we have no obligation to allow these kinds of bad attitudes to have influence upon our life. This was probably a challenging issue for Timothy, since Paul had to address this personally with Timothy (1 Tim. 4:12). He had to bring this up with the church in Corinth as well. When Paul wrote to inform the believers there that Timothy would come to visit them, he brought up this issue (1 Cor. 16:10-11). As we saw in the previous chapter, this kind of fear and intimidation can become a snare that makes us passive. For this reason, Paul wrote to encourage Timothy to stir up the spiritual gifts in his life once again, by breaking the power of fear.

Another challenge for Timothy was the health issues regarding his stomach (1 Tim. 5:23). It is very likely that Timothy had some struggles with his health at times. All of us will have to learn how to handle weakness and personal challenges in our life with God. But as we learn to abide in the love of the Father, we find wisdom in how to process the weak areas of our life in a way that doesn't hinder our walk with God. Here we can see yet another powerful example that illustrates how important it is to have good people in our lives. Paul very actively encouraged Timothy to overcome his weaknesses. We need that type of people in our life, but we also need to be that kind of influence for other people.

Lessons to Learn from Timothy

Seeing that Timothy, who had been blessed with such a beautiful family heritage and the best mentor available, still had a struggle with fear and insecurity should give us a lot of hope. We all have areas of weakness and sometimes we struggle with insecurities and fear. As we have already noticed, the name Timothy means *"dear to God"*. We are our Father's beloved children and we are dear to Him as well. We know that the Father's love casts out all fear. This means that if we're challenged by our insecurities and fear, we can run to the Father. He wants to shower us with His healing love and affection. All fear must leave our lives when the love of the Father is fully revealed in us. Fear will be replaced by a holy boldness and security.

Another lesson we can learn from the life of Timothy, is learning to value and steward our spiritual heritage. We do that by loving and honoring the people that we have received from. The Father can accomplish great things through believers who have humble hearts and are willing to be trained by good mentors (2 Tim. 1:5, 13-14, 2:2, 3:10, 14-15). Timothy was that kind of man and his life still have a powerful impact on the body of Christ. He became an apostle, and he was also a teacher and pastor in Ephesus (1 Tess.

1:1, 2:6). His ministry became very fruitful and his life speaks to us even today. Our Father can accomplish more than we thought possible through the believer whose life has been transformed by the love of the Father. This is the kind of people that we are now growing into!

Activations

- We read Acts 16:1-3 and Phil. 2:19-23 in this chapter. Spend some time reflecting on these passages with the Holy Spirit. Invite Him to provide more insight from these passages, on how we can grow in our sonship. Timothy had the heart of a son. There is much we can learn from his example. Write down the insights that the Holy Spirit reveals to you.

- There are many lessons we can learn, by studying the life and ministry of Timothy. Do some research on his life, by studying the Bible and by communicating with the Holy Spirit. Write down at least three important lessons that you can learn from Timothy's life.

- Timothy inherited a rich spiritual inheritance from his mother and from being mentored by Paul as well. Do you have a similar spiritual inheritance? Who are the mentors that have shaped your life? How can you get a spiritual inheritance? Spend some time in prayer to gain more wisdom in this area.

- Take 20-30 minutes in prayer. Ask the Father for His love to transform your heart, so that you can grow in sonship even more. Timothy was an ordinary young man, with a lot of weaknesses and challenges that he had to overcome. The same is true for us. Invite Jesus to make you an overcomer through His love.

- In this chapter, we discovered that the name Timothy means *Dear to God*. You are very dear to your Father as well. Spend some time soaking in His presence and ask him to shower you with His lovingkindness.

CHAPTER 19: CALLED INTO FELLOWSHIP WITH JESUS CHRIST

Our Father is a relational God. This is one of the reasons why the Trinity is so important to us. The Father's greatest desire is for us to live in experiential union with Christ. *"God is faithful, by whom ye were called unto the fellowship of his Son Jesus Christ our Lord"* (1 *Cor. 1:9).* We will never be able to fully grasp how He can be one God, but yet three persons. The Trinity should never be viewed as just another intellectual, or theological concept for us to study. The trinity is a divine fellowship of love that has become our new and eternal family.

The Father, Jesus the Son, and the Holy Spirit abides in an eternal and everlasting relationship of love, honor, and generosity. This can be clearly seen, by looking at how they are always lifting and honoring one another. The Father sent the Son, because He loves us and wants all of us to come back home. When Jesus came into this world, His focus and mission was to reveal the Father. They then sent the Holy Spirit, who now glorifies Jesus. When Jesus is glorified, He brings us back home to the Father again. The Trinity is a fellowship of self-giving love that is united in an unbreakable bond of honor and generosity. Our Father is a relational God and in giving the great commission, He lets us know that He wants a close, personal relationship with every one of us. Therefore, He has now called us into fellowship with Jesus. This calling is the foundational calling of every believer. Everything else grows out of our relationship with God. Our calling consists of three things, which we will study within this chapter:

1.   *We are called into fellowship with Jesus Christ.*
2.   *We are called to rest.*
3.   *We are called to freedom.*

1. We are Called into Fellowship with Jesus

We find several examples of how Jesus invited people to come to Him in the gospels. He calls us to Himself in the same way today. It's significant that we hear both what Jesus said and didn't say, when He called us into fellowship with Himself. The Bible tells us how Jesus called the disciples to come and follow Him:

And Jesus, walking by the sea of Galilee, saw two brethren, Simon called Peter, and Andrew his brother, casting a net into the sea: for they were fishers. And he saith unto them, follow me, and I will make you fishers of men. And they straightway left their nets, and followed him. And going on from thence, he saw other two brethren, James the son of Zebedee, and John his brother, in a ship with Zebedee their father, mending their nets; and he called them. And they immediately left the ship and their father, and followed him (Matt. 4:18-22).

In this passage, we read about how Jesus called both Simon and Andrew, as well as James and John. He challenged them to come and follow Him. We know that this wasn't the first time that they met Jesus. They had already been introduced to Him, right after His baptism (John 1:35-51). Through this calling, He invited the disciples to deepen their relationship with Him. This calling had two important ingredients:

1. *Come and follow Me.*

The disciples could decide if they wanted to respond to His calling or not, but the call from Jesus was to follow Him. He didn't promise them a big ministry, or that they were to be part of a movement of world changers. Jesus didn't promise them that they would ignite a big revival or become powerful apostles. Jesus simply invited them to follow Himself. I like the raw simplicity of this calling. They were called to join Him, without knowing anything about what would happen next. They had to leave their whole lives in the hands of Jesus, including their dreams, expectations, and their hopes for the future. This call was all about Jesus. It's still all about Christ today, since this same calling has been given to us as well. We have been called into fellowship with Jesus Himself. By getting to know Him, we are brought back home to the Father.

2. *I will make you fishers of men.*

The second part of this calling was that Jesus wanted to transform these disciples into fishers of men. Their part was to say yes to the invitation of Jesus and His part was to transform them into the persons that God had created them to be. This reveals to us that Jesus will personally handle the process, through which He makes us mature sons and daughters. To answer this call is our choice, but once we have said yes and chosen to follow Him, we are predestined to be fully conformed into the image of Jesus (Rom. 8:29). Again, our job is to say yes to that call and Jesus Himself will transform of our lives, shaping us into fishers of men.

Notice what Jesus didn't say. Jesus didn't say that He was calling the disciples into a discipleship program, or a lifelong process of spiritual formation. Neither did Jesus give us seven steps, or ten habits, that will guarantee success if we follow them. He simply called us to Himself. Why? Because to Jesus, having relationship with us is the most important thing. He is not impressed by what we do for Him but Jesus desperately wants our heart. So, He calls us into fellowship with Himself. As our relationship with Jesus develops, it might be expressed by us forming certain habits, or by embracing a set of spiritual disciplines. This give shape to our relationship with Jesus, but the goal will always be to know Him in deeper ways. We are disciples of Jesus and we can only learn from Him by knowing Him.

2.   We are Called to Rest

Are you tired? Worn out? Burned out on religion? Come to me. Get away with me and you'll recover your life. I'll show you how to take a real rest. Walk with me and work with me—watch how I do it. Learn the unforced rhythms of grace. I won't lay anything heavy or ill-fitting on you. Keep company with me and you'll learn to live freely and lightly (Matt. 11:28-30 The Message).

We already looked at this verse in an earlier chapter, but here we will look at it again from a little different perspective. I love how the Message translates this passage. Here, Jesus once again gives an invitation to come to Him. This is an invitation given to people who are tired and burned out on religion. By coming to Jesus, He promises us a beautiful exchange. We will lose our religion and instead get our lost life back. Jesus will show us how to really rest by teaching us the unforced rhythms of grace. When we live in fellowship with Jesus, He promises to teach us how to live freely and lightly, because that is how He does it.

It is important for us to consider the context here. The people that Jesus called to Himself lived in a society, steeped in religion and legalistic practices. All the laws and regulations that they had to remember, would cause anyone who took them seriously, to get tired and worn out. The main difference between the scribes and Jesus, was that while Jesus came to deliver and heal us from the oppression of all legalistic burdens, the scribes were putting such burdens on the people instead. Jesus said that *"…you crush people with unbearable religious demands, and you never lift a finger to ease the burden" (Luke 11:46 NLT).* When we come to Jesus Christ, He reveals the heart of the Father and through that revelation we are delivered from living by religious regulations and laws. We are set free to embrace a lifestyle where we are learning to live by the unforced rhythms of grace.

The Unforced Rhythms of Grace

The grace of God is the transforming power of the gospel. Paul describes how our lives are transformed by the grace of God like this:

For the grace of God that bringeth salvation hath appeared to all men, teaching us that, denying ungodliness and worldly lusts, we should live soberly, righteously, and godly, in this present world; looking for that blessed hope, and the glorious appearing of the great God and our Saviour Jesus Christ; who gave himself for us, that he might redeem us from all iniquity, and purify unto himself a peculiar people, zealous of good works (Tit. 2:11-14).

The grace of God is the power of Jesus operating within us. Grace is His unmerited favor or undeserved goodwill. Grace is also His active empowering, which causes us to fulfill every task that He has prepared for us. His grace operates in such a way that it flows like an unforced rhythm through the lives of all His people. That means that we cannot control how the grace of God operates, but we can learn how to go with the flow. What I mean by that is that as we allow His grace to lead us it will be expressed differently, based on how the Father wants to shape the life of the believer. This is the reason why there is not one set of spiritual disciplines that fits us all.

The Same Grace - Different Expressions

And then, after your brief suffering, the God of all loving grace, who has called you to share in his eternal glory in Christ, will personally and powerfully restore you and make you stronger than ever. Yes, he

*will set you firmly in place and build you up. And he has all the power
needed to do this —forever! Amen (1 Pet. 5:10-11 TPT).*

God doesn't work with all His people in the same way, but how
ever He works on us, the outcome will always be Christlikeness.
Our Father is the God of all loving grace. He will always restore,
strengthen and establish us in His will. But the process He takes
us through to bring us there might look a bit different. There are
several factors that plays a part in how this process will look like,
throughout the different seasons of our life.

- ***Our personality and temperament***
  Our Father knows us better than we know ourselves. He
  wants to have a relationship with us that flows naturally.
  If you are like me, you like to have structure to your day.
  I have daily habits of Bible reading, prayer, and studies.
  The schedule for my days, looks almost the same every
  day. This is very important for me to find fulfilment and
  joy in my fellowship with Jesus. My wife who is much
  more spontaneous than me, would probably consider it
  as a straitjacket, if she tried to walk with the Father like I
  do. The good news is that God never called her to copy
  my relationship with Him. Linda does indeed study the
  Bible and she is always practicing the presence of God.
  I'm constantly inspired and challenged, by watching her
  deep and authentic intimacy with God. But I would still
  go crazy if I tried to live like her, because I need more
  structure to my day. Based on our personalities and the
  persons that God has created us to be, our fellowship
  with Christ will look a little different. The principle is:
  The same grace — different expressions.

- ***Callings and gifts***
  Our different callings and the gifts we have been given
  to steward, will also determine how God is shaping us.

An evangelist will need to be trained differently than a prophet, and a teacher will be trained differently than a pastor. The person who is called to work with homeless people needs a different training than the person who is called to reach influencers or politicians. The Father will provide the right training for us, when we accept the call to be shaped by Him. Again, we can see this principle in action: *The same grace — different expressions.*

- *Seasons of Life*
  We all go through many different seasons of life and our relationship with Jesus will look different, depending on our present season. For example, let's compare a single young man to a mother with three kids. They both have received a calling to live in fellowship with Jesus Christ, but how they are responding to that call will probably be very different. The single young man has the freedom to get up to pray and read the Bible early in the morning. But it's hard to pray in the morning, if you wake with a toddler waiting to get fed next to you, while at the same time the older sibling needs to get up and go to school, and the third one has an appointment with the dentist. So, the mother with three kids needs to find a different way to have quality time with Jesus. There are so many different seasons for us. Sometimes, there will be seasons of grief and at other times comes seasons of happiness. Sometimes life is hard and sometimes there are times of rest. Our Father is not insensitive to our seasons of life. The unforced rhythm of grace keeps on flowing through our lives in a way that works wherever we are in our life. Remember this principle once again: *The same grace — different expressions.*

So far, we have looked at two very important parts of our calling. We are called into fellowship with Jesus Christ and to find rest in His grace. There is one more part of our calling that we need to look at before we end this chapter.

3.   We are Called to Freedom

Stand fast therefore in the liberty wherewith Christ hath made us free, and be not entangled again with the yoke of bondage. Behold, I Paul say unto you, that if ye be circumcised, Christ shall profit you nothing. For I testify again to every man that is circumcised, that he is a debtor to do the whole law. Christ is become of no effect unto you, whosoever of you are justified by the law; ye are fallen from grace (Gal. 5:1).

When we responded to the call from Jesus, a beautiful process of transformation began within us. That transformation will always result in us growing into more freedom. The liberty that we have been given as children of God has been fully given to us through the redemptive work of Christ, which means that we cannot earn it. Our freedom is a gift of grace that has been given to us by God because He is good. He wants us to enjoy the full benefits of this wonderful gift. Because freedom is a word that is now being used everywhere in our culture, and almost always being defined very differently than how God defines it, we need to understand what true freedom is.

Christlikeness Equals Freedom

The true freedom of sonship is to live in a deep revelation of the Father's love for us. We have been created in the image of Jesus Christ, but we have also seen that we are being transformed into His image. This might seem like a contradiction, but it is not. A simple way to describe what this means is that we are becoming who we already are (Rom. 8:29, 2 Cor. 3:17-18). Jesus Christ is the original picture and we have been created in His image. As we're growing in our relationship with the Father, Christ will be more clearly revealed through us. This doesn't mean that we will lose our personality or become a pale copy of someone else. As Jesus is revealed through us, our true selves are also revealed in Him. We become more ourselves when we grow in Christlikeness. The Father uses this process to deliver us from everything in our lives that doesn't look like Jesus. Things like sin, bondages, wounds, condemnation, and oppression must leave us. In other words, we will find true freedom through growing in Christlikeness.

Becoming Who We Already Are

Sometimes we think of Christlikeness only in terms of imitation, meaning that we're reading about Jesus in the gospels and try to imitate His actions. That isn't what Christlikeness is about at all. We need to remember that Jesus didn't call us to fulfill religious programs. Trying to imitate the life of Jesus, would be to sign up for such a program on steroids! Christlikeness means that we are growing into our most authentic selves, by allowing Jesus Christ to be formed within us (Gal. 4:19-20). Our Father doesn't work in the field of behavior modification and self-help. His expert field has always been heart transformation.

Growing in Christlikeness means that we are being set free from everything in our lives that doesn't look like Christ. For example, we don't find any fear, rejection, or insecurity in the life of Jesus. This means that we shouldn't have this in our lives either. I had a wrong understanding of this for a long time, so the thought of becoming like Jesus intimidated me. I knew myself well enough to know that I could never live like Jesus did. So, after years of struggle to become a good christian, I finally just gave up. This was exactly what the Holy Spirit had been waiting for all along. Only by giving up my own efforts could I give Him the necessary space and freedom to transform my heart. It's actually when we stop trying to create a life based on performance that we can start to live by the unforced rhythms of grace. This is a very beautiful journey into true freedom.

God Is Free

All freedom comes from God because He is totally free. There is nothing that oppresses the Father, neither is there anything that binds the Jesus or the Holy Spirit. This might sound self-evident, but the truth is that it's hard for us to grasp how free God really is. It is a constant challenge to realize that the Holy Spirit will not stay in our boxes. Jesus Himself is always so much bigger than all our definitions of Him. Jesus is totally free and part of being transformed into His image is to grow in freedom as well.

Now the Lord is that Spirit: and where the Spirit of the Lord is, there is liberty. But we all, with open face beholding as in a glass the glory of the Lord, are changed into the same image from glory to glory, even as by the Spirit of the Lord (2 Cor. 3:17-18).

In the presence of the Holy Spirit there is true liberty. This is very intimately connected with our transformation. Whenever we live in deep fellowship with the Holy Spirit, the result will always be freedom. Together with Him, we are free to be ourselves. People always reproduce what they carry in their hearts. Our internal culture will always become the culture that we reproduce in our home and relationships. If we are filled with joy and peace, that will be the atmosphere that fills the space we occupy. Since the Spirit of the Lord is free, freedom will always be the atmosphere that He brings with Him and the culture that He will establish if He is welcomed. In the same way, Jesus speaks about the fruit of our fellowship with Him as a growth in freedom.

If you continue in My word, then you are truly My disciples; and you will know the truth, and the truth will set you free." They answered Him, "We are Abraham's descendants and have never been enslaved to anyone; how is it that You say, 'You will become free'?" Jesus answered them, "Truly, truly I say to you, everyone who commits sin is a slave of sin. Now the slave does not remain in the house forever; the son does remain forever. So if the Son sets you free, you really will be free (John 8:31-36 NASB).

Jesus Did Only What He Saw the Father Do

Jesus reveals to us that true freedom is only found in learning to live in dependence on God.

Most assuredly, I say to you, the Son can do nothing of Himself, but what He sees the Father do; for whatever He does, the Son also does in like manner. For the Father loves the Son, and shows Him all things that He Himself does; and He will show Him greater works than these, that you may marvel (John 5:19-20 NKJV).

This was the source of Jesus' life. If we want to be like Christ, we need to be connected to the same source that He was. That source is the heart of the Father. Jesus did only what He saw the Father doing because He always abided in the Father's love. This is how we can live like Jesus and this is how He is being formed within us. That happens as we abide in the love of God, giving up our striving and abandon our hopes of accomplishing intimacy with Christ through our own strength. We grow into the freedom of sonship by abiding in the love of the Father and when Jesus calls us to follow Him, He will always lead us to the Father, where He takes us on a journey deeper into the Father's heart.

Independence Always Equals Bondage

To live in independence is one of the worst bondages there is. It means that we must trust our own strength to figure out our life with the Lord. Jesus showed us a superior way to live with Him. When Jesus commissioned His disciples to preach the gospel, He told them that He was now sending them, in the same way that He was sent by the Father. "*Then said Jesus to them again, Peace be unto you: as my Father hath sent me, even so send I you" (John 20:21).* Just like Jesus live by the life of the Father, so we live by the life of Christ. We no longer need to manage life in our own strength, competence, or ability. We have been invited to fellowship with Jesus Christ, who wants to express His very life through us. We are never alone and will never be left on our own to fix our lives. That is freedom!

Legalism Challenges Our Freedom

The struggle we face is to stand firm in our glorious freedom in Christ. Our freedom will be challenged by religion and legalistic traditions. The world is under the rule of the devil and he doesn't want people to be delivered from his influence (2 Cor. 4:4). We shouldn't think of his influence only in terms of what I like to call "bad" flesh. By that, I mean obvious sins like immorality, lust, or the other works of the flesh (Gal. 5:19-21). What we need to have in mind here is the religious flesh, which I call the "good" flesh. By that, I mean our tendency to try to do our Father's will in our own strength. This is one of the major strongholds in the body of Christ. The religious bondage is so deceptive precisely because it appears like zeal for God, but it always leads us into even more bondage. Flesh is still flesh, no matter how good it may appear.

The appearance of goodness only makes it more deceptive. This deception operates by suggesting that we need to become more holy to live in a strong relationship with God. This is a deception. Since Satan knows that this has been a successful strategy, this is usually the way he operates. The truth is that we have been made free in Christ. We already have a perfect standing with the Father right now. We are now growing in that relationship, but abiding in the Father's love transforms us, based on the finished work of Christ, but never through our performance. The devil knows that he has no power over our relationship with the Father. He uses deception to bring us back under the burden of religion. If we are fooled by his deceptive tactics, we end up under a cloud of guilt, that causes us to lose connection with the love of the Father.

Religious Deception

The deception of the devil is so tricky because he is using a well-known, yet unexpected tactic. In this passage Paul describes how Satan deceives the believer into religious bondage:

But I fear, lest by any means, as the serpent beguiled Eve through his subtilty, so your minds should be corrupted from the simplicity that is in Christ… And no marvel; for Satan himself is transformed into an angel of light. Therefore it is no great thing if his ministers also be transformed as the ministers of righteousness; whose end shall be according to their works. (2 Cor. 11:3, 14-15).

Satan comes to us as the angel of light, which means that he uses religious deception to deceive us by pretending to be the voice of God. His goal is to steal our attention so that we are distracted away from the simplicity of abiding in Christ. As we saw earlier in this chapter, Jesus calls us to Himself in a very simple way. We are called to come into fellowship with Him. We should always remember that the gospel is simple and life in intimacy with the Father is so simple that it is available to anyone. Religion wants to complicate our relationship with God, so that we disqualify ourselves from abiding in His presence, sensing that we have not done enough to qualify. This will bind us in condemnation. The simplicity of the gospel liberates us from performance-based and complicated religious programs. It brings us into union with the Father through the grace provided for us in Christ. Every child of God can walk in a simple intimacy with the Father and in the fullness of His blessings.

Stand Firm in Freedom

We stand firm in freedom by continually keeping our focus fixed on Jesus Christ and by abiding in the love of the Father. The Holy Spirit is helping us by continually pouring the Father's love into our hearts, and by revealing the glory of Jesus Christ (Rom 5:5, 2 Cor. 3:17-18). As we have already seen, this is how we find true delivered from the bondage of religion. Jesus didn't come to start a new religion, or to impose a complicated religious program on His followers. He simply called us to Himself, so that He could bring us home to the Father.

Activations

- We studied 1 Cor. 1:9 in this chapter. Spend some time reflecting on this verse with Jesus. Invite Him to give more insight to you, on how you can grow in intimacy with Him. Write down what Jesus reveals to you.

- For a deeper insight into how you can respond to this glorious calling into fellowship with Jesus Christ, read my book, *Partnering with the Love of Christ.* This book is all about how you can respond to this calling.

- Within this chapter we saw how we are called to three things as believers. These three things are:

  1. *We are called into fellowship with Jesus Christ.*
  2. *We are called to rest.*
  3. *We are called to freedom.*

  How can you respond to these three callings? Is there any of these callings that you need to grow more in? Can you see any growth in any of these three areas? Invite the Holy Spirit to speak to you on this topic. Write down what He reveals to you.

- Take 20-30 minutes in prayer. Respond to the calling into fellowship with Jesus. Express your love to Him. Then ask Him to reveal more of His heart to you, and invite Him to transform you by His grace.

- Take some time in intercession for the body of Christ. Ask the Father to bring us deeper into intimacy with His Son. Then ask Him to conform us after the image of His Son, so that Jesus can be revealed through His body in an even more glorious way.

CHAPTER 20: COMFORT AND ENCOURAGEMENT FROM GOD

We have an everlasting ocean of comfort and encouragement to drink from, through our fellowship with the Father. In fact, Paul describes how receiving comfort and encouragement from Jesus Christ, is the only way to live in unity and selfless love. The good news is that in Christ, we always have an endless source of both.

Therefore if you have any encouragement from being united with Christ, if any comfort from his love, if any common sharing in the Spirit, if any tenderness and compassion, then make my joy complete by being like-minded, having the same love, being one in spirit and of one mind (Phil. 2:1-4 NIV).

Encouragement and comfort from the Father are at the core of our relationship with Him. He wants to create an internal culture of comfort and encouragement within our heart. Both the Father, Jesus, and the Holy Spirit longs to comfort us continually and to fill our lives with heavenly encouragement. God is the ultimate encourager, which is the reason that He gave prophetic ministry to us. The prophetic is meant to strengthen the body of Christ by speaking words of comfort and encouragement to the bride: *"But one who prophesies strengthens others, encourages them, and comforts them"* (1 Cor. 14:3 NLT). It is important that we realize that being encouraged is the fruit of having been comforted. A person who has been mourning, but then receives comfort from God will be full of encouragement as well. It would be a mistake to think that a believer who flows in encouragement never have experienced any suffering. Such a believer is rather someone who have been suffering and mourning but has learned to come to the Father to be comforted. Encouragement is the fruit that always grows from the comfort we have received in our fellowship with the Father.

The God of All Comfort

We find one example of the power of comfort in 2 Corinthians, where Paul describes his own experiences of being comforted by the Father during times of pain and suffering:

Praise be to the God and Father of our Lord Jesus Christ, the Father of compassion and the God of all comfort, who comforts us in all our troubles, so that we can comfort those in any trouble with the comfort we ourselves receive from God. For just as we share abundantly in the sufferings of Christ, so also our comfort abounds through Christ. If we are distressed, it is for your comfort and salvation; if we are comforted, it is for your comfort, which produces in you patient endurance of the same sufferings we suffer (2 Cor. 1:3-6 NIV).

This is how Paul opened his letter to the Corinthian church. This was a very interesting way of starting this letter, considering that his apostolic ministry was challenged and that his leadership had been called into question. We saw earlier how some people in the Corinthian church had lost all their trust in Paul and his ministry. They doubted him precisely because they didn't view him as the strong leader that they expected a man of God and a pioneering apostle to be. Of course, knowing that Paul's main goal here was to redefine what spiritual strength is, maybe we shouldn't be that surprised. Paul defines spiritual strength as depending on God's grace and power, operating through our weaknesses. Paul shares how he could endure the many sufferings he experienced while being on his missionary journeys. He found all the strength He needed in fellowshipping with the Father of compassion, who is the God of all comfort. He didn't have to handle all his challenges and pain by himself. He ran to the Father and abiding in His love became Paul's secure stronghold of comfort and encouragement. He lived by the words that Jesus had spoken to him: *"My grace is sufficient for thee: for my strength is made perfect in weakness"* (2 Cor. 12:9). These words were bread of life for Paul.

Paul Was No Super Apostle

There is a risk when reading about Paul, that we misunderstand who he was and as a result, don't understand his message to us. If we do that, we could fall into the religious myth that paints the picture of Paul as the superhuman apostle, who was tougher and stronger than the rest of us. In fact, this is the misunderstanding that Paul is trying to correct here. Paul wasn't strong because he was more competent or disciplined than the rest of us. He found his strength by abiding in the love of the Father. Paul had learned to run to the throne of grace to receive grace in his times of need, which turned out to be most of the time for him. That's how Paul found the strength to walk through the trials and sufferings that he had to face. He knew the God of all comfort!

If we make the same mistake as the Corinthians, by believing that spiritual strength is about being strong in ourselves, we will end up confusing true spiritual strength with a strong or charismatic personality. This is the reason that Paul took every opportunity to boast about His weaknesses. He wrote: *"If boasting is necessary, I will boast about examples of my weakness. The God and Father of the Lord Jesus, who is eternally praised, knows that I am speaking the truth" (2 Cor. 11:30-31 TPT).* He gladly boasted in his weaknesses because he knew that it was in the places of personal weakness, that he found true spiritual strength through the grace of God. In fact, Paul was very transparent in both letters to the Corinthians and it seems that He did that on purpose, just to give an example of true spiritual strength. That strength is found in knowing God as the source of our encouragement and comfort.

Our Comforter

When Jesus describes the ministry of the Holy Spirit, He is saying that the Holy Spirit is our comforter, who will always abide with us: *"But the Comforter, which is the Holy Ghost, whom the Father will send in my name, he shall teach you all things, and bring all things to your remembrance, whatsoever I have said unto you" (John 14:26).* It's a big part of the ministry of the Holy Spirit to be our comforter. The Holy Spirit is our teacher, but it is important that we realize not just what He teaches us, but also in what way He does it. The Holy Spirit is our intercessor and advocate, who is speaking on our behalf. He is witnessing to our hearts, by convicting us of our identity in Christ. He encourages us by reminding us that we are the righteousness of God in Christ. In this way, the Holy Spirit is comforting our hearts. The Holy Spirit is always there to help us in our weaknesses by encouraging us. He is doing that by always reminding us of the victory that Jesus Christ won for us. *"Likewise the Spirit also helps in our weaknesses. For we do not know what we should pray for as we ought, but the Spirit Himself makes intercession for us with groanings which cannot be uttered (Rom. 8:26 NKJV).* The Holy Spirit always intercedes for us by pleading our case, as our advocate and comforter. He constantly reminds us of our true identity in Christ and strengthens us by unveiling Jesus to us. He shows us that has defeated the devil and the powers of evil. Jesus speaks about the Holy Spirit's ministry as our helper, encourager and comforter within this passage:

And when he is come, he will reprove the world of sin, and of righteousness, and of judgment: of sin, because they believe not on me; of righteousness, because I go to my Father, and ye see me no more; of judgment, because the prince of this world is judged (John 16:8-11).

The Holy Spirit convicts the world of sin to show them that they need Jesus, but for us as believers, the ministry of the Holy Spirit works very different. He will comfort us by revealing two things that is of vital importance, if we want to build an internal culture of comfort and encouragement:

1. *He reminds us of our righteousness in Christ.*
   It's part of His ministry to remind us of our true identity as children of God and to reveal the inheritance that we have received in Christ. We need daily reminders of this and the Holy Spirit is the one who does this reminding. He reveals who we are in Christ. When life is tough and our circumstances and feelings speaks all kinds of mixed messages to us, the Spirit is there to remind us of our real identity, as the beloved and favored children of God.

2. *He reminds us that the devil is defeated.*
   Another important part of the Holy Spirit's ministry is to remind us of the complete victory of Christ. Jesus has defeated the devil and all the power of darkness in a total and complete way. Even if things look bad in the world and evil seems to be triumphing in our lives at times, the truth is that the devil has been defeated on the cross. We need to be reminded of this every day of our lives. Jesus has defeated every spiritual attack that comes against us!

These two truths will establish our hearts in the victory of Christ. They reveal our identity as children of God, who are more than conquerors through Him who loves us. Jesus is now triumphant and we are his victorious brothers and sisters. We have received a new identity as children and heirs of God. The Holy Spirit have helped me through some very challenging seasons, by convicting my heart this way. As my family and I have responded to the call of God, we have sometimes walked through some more narrow passages in our life with Jesus. These includes spiritual attacks, financial challenges and even life-threatening situations. During these seasons, the Holy Spirit has comforted us and we have been able to stay encouraged and focused on our calling.

It's not only during the tougher seasons of life that the Holy Spirit comforts us. I have made it my daily habit to let Him speak into my heart, witnessing about my identity in Christ and the victory of Jesus. We need daily reminders that every spiritual attack has been defeated on the cross. Therefore, we already know that we will win in every battle!

The Tragedy of Not Finding Comfort

There is a passage in the book of Ecclesiastes that addresses the tragedy of being stuck in a life of pain, suffering and oppression, when there is no comfort or healing available. The words that we read in this powerful passage describes the soul of the western world, where loneliness has become like an epidemic of its own:

So I returned, and considered all the oppressions that are done under the sun: and behold the tears of such as were oppressed, and they had no comforter; and on the side of their oppressors there was power; but they had no comforter. Wherefore I praised the dead which are already dead more than the living which are yet alive. Yea, better is he than both they, which hath not yet been, who hath not seen the evil work that is done under the sun (Eccl. 4:1-3).

This also describes the inner life of many of the people who come to me for prayer and counseling. These people have heard about the power of God, and they know His promises concerning their healing and deliverance. But their hearts are still broken and full of pain because they haven't learned to come to God for comfort. When a person has been living long enough with a heart full of pain, they will start to see life as a torment or even a curse. That's not a view of life that Jesus wants us to have. He came to give us abundant life and He wants us to be able to fully enjoy life as the tremendous gift that it truly is. That is impossible when pain and oppression clouds our vision.

The Blessing of Mourning in the Father's Arms

It is very hard to find hope and vision for change and for a better future, if we have nowhere to run with our pain and grief. This is the reason that Jesus made this statement: *"Blessed are those who mourn, for they will be comforted" (Matt. 5:4).* As children of God, we have truly been blessed. We have the wonderful privilege of having instant access to the Father's comforting love. He always welcomes us with open arms, whenever we need to run to Him. Being comforted by the Father is not hard work. We can come to Him with our pain and speak to Him about it. Then we leave the heartache and disappointments of life there with Him. The only thing we need to do is to live open and authentic lives before the Father, allowing His grace to be our strength.

Learning to Receive Comfort from God

One of the main reasons why it is so hard for believers to receive comfort from the Father, is simply because they haven't thought of prayer in this way before. It's very common that people relate to prayer only in terms of coming to God get an answer, or in the terms of intercession and spiritual warfare. These are good and important parts of a believer's prayer life, but it's also important to realize that sometimes the solution isn't in finding a solution. Sometimes, the real need is to just talk to God about our pain and abide in the Father's healing love. Some of the most comforting and encouraging experiences of my life has happened when I just shared my deep pain and sorrow with a friend who just listened. This has been even more true in my relationship with my Father.

A couple of years before I wrote this book, I had a series of deeper encounters with the Father's comforting love. The love that these encounters imparted into my heart, went deeper than anything I had ever experienced before. I had always been both comforted and encouraged by spending time with Him, but during the time of these encounters, I walked through a season of pain that was almost unbearable. During this season, receiving His comforting love became much more real to me than it had been ever before. I kept running to the Father and He kept embracing me with His love. He never spoke to me or gave me any solution to my pains and problems. He was simply being there for me, listening to the cries of my heart and sharing my pain, until I had wept it all out of my system. After that time of comfort, something had shifted within my heart. The best way I can describe it, is that the internal culture of my heart has been filled with heavenly encouragement and comfort.

There are some verses in the book of Isaiah, that puts into words my experiences with the Father's deep comforting love: *"Sing, O heavens! Be joyful, O earth! And break out in singing, O mountains! For the Lord has comforted His people, and will have mercy on His afflicted"* (Isa. 49:13 NKJV). Experiencing the mercy and comfort of the Father is one of the most powerful experiences I have ever had in all my life. Our Father longs to comfort and encourage His children. *"For the Lord will comfort Zion, He will comfort all her waste places; He will make her wilderness like Eden, and her desert like the garden of the Lord; joy and gladness will be found in it, thanksgiving and the voice of melody"* (Isa. 51:3 NKJV).

God's Longing to Comfort His People

There is a deep longing within the heart of God, to comfort and encourage His people. The Father, Jesus and the Holy Spirit want us to come to them with our pains and struggles. We can safely break down in our Father's arms to receive comfort and healing from Him. *"Comfort ye, comfort ye my people, saith your God. Speak ye comfortably to Jerusalem, and cry unto her, that her warfare is accomplished, that her iniquity is pardoned: for she hath received of the LORD's hand double for all her sins"* (Isi. 40:1-2). The throne of God is a throne of grace, where we can run to find mercy and grace in our time of need (Hebr. 4:16). We are invited to come boldly to Him. The Father is longing to help us and He wants us to count on His power to work on our behalf. We often emphasize how to receive miracles and breakthroughs from God, but we must also understand that God is more passionate for this to happen, than we could ever hope to become. The Father really loves us and He wants us to grow into our full purpose and destiny.

The Power of Encouragement

There is power to overcome and endure in receiving encouraging words from heaven. Heavenly encouragement could either come from the Father directly, or it will come through another believer. An encouraging culture keeps our hearts soft. *"But encourage one another every day, as long as it is still called "today," so that none of you will be hardened by the deceitfulness of sin" (Hebr. 3:13 NASB).* As we have already noted earlier in this chapter, when we have been comforted, our hearts will be filled with encouragement as well. This will provide renewed vision and hope for our lives and future. Both are fruits of having been encouraged by the Father. There is great power in heavenly encouragement. Proverbs tells us: *"A merry heart doeth good like a medicine: But a broken spirit drieth the bones" (Prov. 17:22).* The true encouragement from Jesus fills us with joy and a joyful heart is good medicine for our whole being.

Living in discouragement will make us feel dry and hopeless in our lives with God. It makes us hard and cynical. As children of God, we should have a soft and moldable heart before Him. One of the ways that we keep our hearts soft to God and free from the deception of sin, is to receive our daily dose of encouragement from God. Oftentimes when we are tempted to lose our focus or to let go of our visions, it is because of hopelessness. It causes us to feel that our lives are not making a difference. It's during times like that we need to let our hearts be filled with encouragement.

Jesus is an amazing encourager. I have never had an encounter with Him that left me hopeless and despairing. It is always very encouraging and inspiring to spend time together with Jesus. In His presence, there is always an abundance of encouragement.

The Father has even given a specific ministry of encouragement to the body of Christ (Rom. 12:8). We are going to end this book by studying the life of a man who was a very powerful example of how the ministry of encouragement can be expressed through our lives. This man operated in a ministry of encouragement and comfort. He sets a powerful example for everyone who longs to minister comfort and encouragement to the children of God. His ministry reflects much of what the life of abiding in the Father's love will look like.

Activations

- We studied Phil. 2:1-4 and 2 Cor. 1:3-6, in this chapter. Spend some time reflecting on these passages with the Father. Invite Him to give more insight to you on how you can receive comfort and encouragement from His heart. Write down what He reveals to you.

- We read about the tragedy of a life, where there is no comfort from Eccl. 4:1-3. How does it affect your life as a believer, if you haven't learned how to receive the Father's comfort? Are you good at receiving comfort from Him? Does something hinder you from drinking in His comfort right now? Spend some time reflecting upon this passage and these questions with the Holy Spirit. Write down the revelations you receive.

- We noted that the whole Trinity is very passionate to comfort and encourage us. Spend some time in prayer and invite them to minister comforting love to you:

  1. *The Father (2 Cor. 1:3-6)*
  2. *Jesus (Phil. 2:1-4)*
  3. *The Holy Spirit (John 16:8-11)*

  Spend 20-30 minutes with each one of them, soaking in their love while asking them to comfort and speak encouragement to your heart. You can use the passage that I have written here as a foundation, while you're praying.

- Spend time in intercession for the body of Christ. Ask the Father to comfort and encourage His children, and to equip us to minister heavenly encouragement and comfort to everyone who needs it.

CHAPTER 21: BARNABAS - THE MINISTRY OF ENCOURAGEMENT

The book of Acts provides a biblical blueprint for life in the Spirit, church life and missions. In this book, we read about some of the early apostles. Barnabas was one of these apostles. I have always been very fascinated by his ministry and the way he operated in the early church. He wasn't the most visible or well-known of the apostles, but his influence as a mentor and encourager who could see beyond past struggles and help people to grow in Christ was powerful. In this chapter, we're going to learn some valuable and helpful lessons, by studying the life of Barnabas and his ministry as a mentor and encourager. He brought a lot of encouragement and comfort to some people and churches, that later became very powerful influencers and leaders within the early church. I have always believed that the ministry of comfort and encouragement is one of the most important fruits that grows from a lifestyle of abiding in the Father's love. We're now going to study the life of Barnabas, to learn more about this wonderful ministry (For more on this ministry, read my book, *The Burning Love of Jesus Christ*).

Who was Barnabas?

Now Joseph, a Levite of Cyprian birth, who was also called Barnabas by the apostles (which translated means Son of Encouragement), owned a tract of land. So he sold it, and brought the money and laid it at the apostles' feet (Acts 4:36-37 NASB).

Barnabas real name was Joseph and he was a levite from Cyprus. Most likely, the reason that he was called Barnabas was because of his character and the way he ministered. Barnabas means son of encouragement, but if we look at the literal meaning we find that his name means son of *Nabas* (i.e. prophecy). Since one of the main goals of the gift of prophecy is to encourage, both meanings of his name work well. In many ways, Barnabas' ministry reveals the heart of New Covenant prophetic ministry. It is obvious that the church in Jerusalem held Barnabas in a high esteem and they trusted him a lot. We can see this from the way they trusted his discernment concerning the conversion of Paul (Acts 9:26-28). It was Barnabas who was sent to Antioch, to strengthen and build up the newly established church there (Acts 11:22). His ministry as an encourager was needed in situations like these. He also had a mercy-motivated personality, which is proven by how quick he was to forgive and restore believers that had failed.

A Good Man, Full of the Holy Spirit and of Faith

Barnabas was an encourager, but he was also described as a good man full of the Holy Spirit and faith. *"For he was a good man, full of the Holy Spirit and of faith. And a great many people were added to the Lord" (Acts 11:24).* These character traits should be present in a Spirit-filled life because it is by abiding in the presence of God that our faith and the fruit of the spirit grows (Eph. 1:17-21, Gal. 5:22-23). Such a lifestyle creates a heavenly balance that produces a fruitful and lasting ministry. This is the reason Paul encourages us to continually be filled with the Spirit (Eph. 5:18-21). The good news is that in Christ, we are now able to live in a constant and instant connection with the Holy Spirit, which means that we can always live full of the presence of God (1 Thess. 5:16-18).

Leadership Based on Identity

It's very interesting to note how Barnabas' leadership was purely based on the man he had become, by being shaped through his intimate relationship with the Father. We often relate to ministry and leadership in terms of vision, gifts, or accomplishments, but Barnabas is being described as a good man full of the Holy Spirit and as the son of encouragement. This tells us much more about his character, than it does about his visions or accomplishments.

I believe that there is an extremely important lesson to learn here. Christlikeness and our character are always more important than our personal charisma or gifts of leadership. When our lives have been shaped by the love of the Father, we will always influence the people that He has placed in our lives. This kind of leadership comes from our surrender to God, where we allow ourselves to be shaped by encountering the heart of the Father.

Barnabas as a Mentor and Encourager

Barnabas was one of the prophets and teachers in Antioch, who were leading the church there. As him and Paul was sent on their mission trip, he was referred to as an apostle as well:

Now there were in the church that was at Antioch certain prophets and teachers; as Barnabas, and Simeon that was called Niger, and Lucius of Cyrene, and Manaen, which had been brought up with Herod the tetrarch, and Saul (Acts 13:1).

But when the apostles Barnabas and Paul... (Acts 14:14 NASB).

Even though Barnabas operated in all these ministries, his most important achievements might have been what he accomplished as a mentor and encourager (Rom. 12:8). Look at these important people that Barnabas mentored throughout his ministry:

- ***The church at Antioch.*** This church became a very strong apostolic church and an important center for missions. It became a center of renewal within the early church.

- ***The apostle Paul,*** who became a pioneering missionary that brought the gospel to the gentile world and he wrote most of the New Testament letters. He has impacted the christian faith more than almost anyone else, except for Jesus himself.

- *John Mark,* who was the son of Barnabas' sister, and the author of the gospel of Mark.

Through the people that Barnabas had mentored, his life became very fruitful. In fact, whenever we read the epistles of Paul and the gospel of Mark, his ministry still bears fruit in our lives today through the impact he had on these men. Barnabas is an example of how we can have a powerful impact for the kingdom of God, by believing in the people that God has put in our lives. All of us can comfort, encourage and pray for people. In this way, we can help them to overcome the past, as well as helping them to reach their full potential in God (Hebr. 3:12-15). We might never know who the people we invest in will grow into once they grow up in Christ. Our encouragement and prayers are very important if we want to see people grow.

Let's look at some examples of how Barnabas mentored people. We begin by studying how Barnabas took Paul under his wings. Paul is mentioned with two different names in the book of Acts. One of these names is Paul, which was his Greek name. The other name is Saul, which was his Jewish name. The book of Acts uses his Jewish name until the ninth verse of chapter thirteen. To not create any confusion, I will do that as well until we have reached that point in the story. Then I will be using his Greek name, just like the book of Acts does.

Barnabas Took Saul under His Wings

When Saul showed up in Jerusalem claiming that he had been born again, the church was very suspicious of him, but Barnabas found a way to reach out to him. After spending some time with Saul, talking to him and questioning him thoroughly, Barnabas found that the testimony of Saul was genuine. So, he brought him before the apostles:

But Barnabas took him and brought him to the apostles. And he declared to them how he had seen the Lord on the road, and that He had spoken to him, and how he had preached boldly at Damascus in the name of Jesus. So he was with them at Jerusalem, coming in and going out (Acts 9:27-28).

Barnabas was a trusted man among the leaders in the Jerusalem and he arranged a meeting with Peter and James. They were still a bit suspicious, but they finally agreed to meet with Saul. It took a lot of courage for Barnabas to bring Paul before the apostles. He took a huge risk by doing that, because if this had been a trap, it would probably have been the end for the church in Jerusalem, not to mention that the lives of James and Peter would have been in grave danger, but this was no trap. In fact, the meeting was so successful that it resulted in Paul being able to walk freely among them, and he even started to preach (Acts 9:28-30). The apostles confirmed that Saul's conversion was genuine. This meeting laid the foundation for Saul's future ministry, since it gave credibility to his testimony. This was one of the most important events in all the book of Acts, and it points to the level of trust that the leaders showed Barnabas. Because Barnabas took time to meet with Saul and listen to his testimony, this important relationship between Saul and the Jerusalem church were established. This friendship shaped the early church and built a bridge between the believers in Jerusalem and the gentile believers.

This situation is a great example of how powerfully the ministry of comfort and encouragement can operate among us. We should never underestimate the power of our key relationships. It's hard to find a more important relationship in the early church, than the divine connection between Paul and Peter. I have seen this in my own life as well. When I got saved, my life was a big mess. I am eternally grateful that some friends of mine could look past this mess, to discern the calling that was hidden beneath all the sin and pain within my life. They became my Barnabas, who comforted and encouraged me. Because they did this, my past has been redeemed and I can now see it in a new light.

A Broken Past in a New Light

Because of the persecution instigated by Saul, the believers were scattered from Jerusalem. As a result, the first gentile church ever was planted in Antioch (Acts 11:19-21). It's interesting to observe how already before his conversion, Saul unconsciously played a part in what later would become his life's mission. He was called to be an apostle to the gentiles and by the persecution that he was leading against the church, the believers were spread out all over the Roman empire. Some of these believers started to preach and they began to minister to the gentiles as well. This was how the gospel began to spread throughout the Roman empire. When we give our broken past to the Father, we will be healed and we can then see our past in a new light. When that happens, our Father make all things work for our good who loves Him, which means that even our scars and brokenness can serve His purposes. This is what happened to Saul here and it's going to happen with our lives as well, if we give our past to the Father.

Barnabas Is Sent to Antioch

A new church with gentile members was established in Antioch. How did the church in Jerusalem react to that? The book of Acts lets us know:

Then news of these things came to the ears of the church in Jerusalem, and they sent out Barnabas to go as far as Antioch. When he came and had seen the grace of God, he was glad, and encouraged them all that with purpose of heart they should continue with the Lord (Acts 11:22-23).

Barnabas traveled to Antioch and he rejoiced when he saw what the grace of God had accomplished among them. He encouraged them to continue to build their intimacy with Jesus. This should be our response as well, if we meet other churches and ministries that are growing. Barnabas didn't want to control or hinder the work of the Holy Spirit among them. All church history reveals that once the leaders try to control what God is doing, the work of the Holy Spirit is quenched. Barnabas didn't do that. Instead, he kept encouraging and supporting the church in Antioch, and he even stayed with them to strengthen their life in Christ.

This church became the center of christianity for years to come. Barnabas' ministry of encouragement laid the foundation for that to happen. Just like Barnabas, we can also strengthen people in a powerful way, by celebrating their victories and encourage them in their work or vision. When we meet other believers, churches, or ministries, it's important not to judge by appearance. If we can discern the prophetic potential that the Father has placed within them, we can help many people to reach their next level in Christ.

Barnabas Shares His Platform with Saul

The work in Antioch kept on growing to the point that Barnabas realized that it had become too big for him to handle by himself. He understood that he needed help, so He came to think about Saul. Barnabas traveled to Tarsus to find him and when he did, he invited him to become a co-worker in Antioch.

Then Barnabas departed for Tarsus to seek Saul. And when he had found him, he brought him to Antioch. So it was that for a whole year they assembled with the church and taught a great many people. And the disciples were first called Christians in Antioch (Acts 11:25-26).

Barnabas found Saul and made him his partner and a leader in Antioch. Barnabas remembered their time together in Jerusalem, and the call he had seen on Saul's life. He brought Saul back to Antioch and they had a fruitful year of ministry there. This laid the foundation for Saul's future apostolic ministry. We need a lot of secure and generous leaders who, just like Barnabas, invest in people and provide opportunities to grow in ministry.

Paul Becomes the Leader

When Saul became known as Paul the apostle and grew into the man that God had called him to be, he quickly became the leader and main preacher of this company (Acts 13:9, 13, 16, 14:12). This wasn't a problem for Barnabas. Being the encourager, his passion was to see people grow. When Paul stepped forth into leadership he could take a step back. This is an important characteristic of a good mentor. We need to discern when it is time to step forward and lead, but also when it's wise to take a step back to give space for the people that we have invested in to grow. Both aspects of leadership are very important. Because Barnabas possessed that wisdom, he knew when to do both.

Barnabas and John Mark

John Mark was the cousin of Barnabas (Col. 4:10). He later wrote the gospel of Mark, but he joined Barnabas and Paul on their first mission trip. *"And Barnabas and Saul returned from Jerusalem when they had fulfilled their ministry, and they also took with them John whose surname was Mark" (Acts 12:25).* John Mark abandoned the team in Perga and went back to Jerusalem (Acts 13:13). We don't know why he left them, but Paul lost his confidence in John Mark because of this. Barnabas, on the other hand, saw the calling of God upon his life and he gave him a second chance (Acts 15:37-40). That turned out to be the right decision. John Mark grew by this experience and he became a valuable co-worker to Barnabas, and later to Peter as well (1 Pet. 5:13). Later in Paul's life, he and John Mark reconciled and worked together again (2 Tim. 4:11).

It is easy to see that the way Barnabas was prepared to trust both Paul and John Mark, laid a strong foundation for future ministry in their lives. When we honor people by trusting them, we create space for them to grow in Christ. One of the ways to encourage people is by choosing to trust in them, even though we know that their track record isn't perfect. They might even have failed us in the past, but God wants us to look beyond that to see their calling and potential in Christ. We must remember that redemption is a big thing to God. It is one of the strongest characteristics of the heart of God. It is important that we learn to look at our brothers and sisters who have failed with eyes of redemption, so that we can believe and work toward their restoration in Christ.

Religious Pressure and an Unresolved Conflict

Barnabas, like the rest of us, was not a man without mistakes and failures. It's very liberating that the Bible doesn't hide the flaws of our heroes of faith. They were ordinary humans just like us. When the religious Jews from Jerusalem came to Antioch, hoping to introduce their legalistic teachings there, Peter withdrew from eating with the gentile believers because of fear (Gal. 2:11-12). All the other Jews that were present, including Barnabas, were also carried away with their hypocrisy. *"And the rest of the Jews also played the hypocrite with him, so that even Barnabas was carried away with their hypocrisy" (Gal. 2:13).* Religious teachings always create fear and separation because of the absence of the love of God.

We can always spot legalism, by recognizing that it creates fear in the heart of people and seduces them away from their freedom in Christ. One of the ways religious teachings accomplishes this, is by calling the believer into a religious type of holiness that is motivated by guilt and the fear of not being good enough. Even Barnabas was among those who reacted with religious fear. Paul confronted Peter in front of the whole church and both Peter and Barnabas repented. It might seem like this was a very drastic step by Paul, but by choosing to not eat with the gentiles, both Peter and Barnabas sent a message that could have ruined everything that God was doing among the gentile believers there. This was more than just adhering to jewish culture. To go back under these regulations and laws from the Old Covenant, directly challenged the gospel Paul preached. The freedom of the children of God was at stake and Paul needed to defend the glorious freedom that Christ had purchased for us. Barnabas repented and there was a reconciliation between him and Paul, but the question is if their relationship had been ruined permanently because of this?

The Weaknesses of Barnabas

That Barnabas couldn't handle the religious pressure in Antioch, might reveal something about his weaknesses. Because Barnabas was the son of encouragement and comfort, his motivational gift and longing was to listen to people and show mercy. Sometimes, those of us who are gifted in this way, can become generous and understanding, to the point that we compromise with truth. Paul realized that this wasn't the time for that type of compromise and understanding. This was a battle for our freedom in Christ and it was good that Paul had the courage and love, to confront Peter and Barnabas in this situation.

The authors of the Bible were very open with the weaknesses and challenges, that the leaders in the early church were struggling with. This gives us good hope for today. It also reminds us of one of the most important truths of the gospel. This truth is that our weaknesses is a gateway for His grace. It is there that His power is revealed the most.

Barnabas and Paul Part Ways

The partnership between Barnabas and Paul ended because they were unable to agree about what to do with John Mark. Barnabas wanted to bring him on their next missionary trip, but Paul did not like that idea. He lost his trust in John Mark, when he had left them during their first trip. They had a heated argument over it:

Barnabas wanted to take John, called Mark, along with them also. But Paul was of the opinion that they should not take along with them this man who had deserted them in Pamphylia and had not gone with them to the work. Now it turned into such a sharp disagreement that they separated from one another, and Barnabas took Mark with him and sailed away to Cyprus. But Paul chose Silas, and left after being entrusted by the brothers to the grace of the Lord (Acts 15:37-40 NASB)

This is the last time we read about Barnabas in the book of Acts, and it ends with him and Paul parting ways over John Mark. We don't know if they ever reconciled, or if they ever met again. It is not necessary to choose side in this conflict. It is enough that we note that Paul and Barnabas had very different personalities and callings. Therefore, they saw the situation concerning John Mark differently. They couldn't settle this conflict and as a result, they parted ways. Barnabas and Mark went to Cyprus, while Paul and Silas went in another direction. The good news is that the Father turned this failure into something good, because He now could work with two powerful apostolic teams instead of one.

It is encouraging to me to read about events like this, because just like Barnabas and Paul, we have failed and made mistakes along the way as well. If we surrender our shortcomings to the Father, He makes them work together for our good (Rom 8:25-28). He is our Healer and He has provided restoration for all our failures so that they can become a steppingstone into greater glory (Rom. 5:20). Not all of us can be the main leader or a pioneering apostle, but all of us can determine to be a positive influence for the Lord on the people that God has placed in our lives. We can learn to be encouragers that see beyond a broken past and strengthen the people we meet, to reach their full potential in Christ. This is one of the lessons we can learn from Barnabas.

Summary

By reading this part of the book, we have studied how knowing the Father's love changes our lives as believers. In fact, it affects every area of our lives in a very dramatic way. Throughout these pages, I wanted to highlight some of the more important aspects of His love in our lives. The important thing is not to seek change for the sake of change, but to get to know the love of the Father. That will automatically change our lives in. One of the things that will emerge out of getting to know His heart, is that the ministry of comfort and encouragement is released through our lives. This is a kind of prophetic ministry and we are called to be a prophetic people. When we start to operate in this ministry, many will be comforted and encouraged to step into everything that God has for them!

Activations

- We studied Acts 4:36-37 and Acts 11:24 in this chapter. Spend some time reflecting on these passages with the Holy Spirit. Invite Him to give more revelation from these passages, to help you grow more in the ministry of comfort and encouragement. Write down what He reveals to you.

- To learn more about the ministry of encouragement, read chapter 19 in my book, *The Burning Love of Jesus Christ*. That chapter is called, *The Encouraging Love of Jesus Christ*, and it reveals more about this ministry.

- We noted how the ministry of Barnabas was built on the man he had become by being conformed into the image of Christ. Why is it important that ministry is built on who we are? What's the biggest differences between a gift-based leadership, compared to the kind of leadership that is built on our relationship with the Father? Spend some time to reflect on this. Invite the Holy Spirit to reveal more on this topic to you. Write down the insights you receive.

- Do your own Bible study and research on the life and ministry of Barnabas. Read all the Scriptures that you can find about his life. Invite the Holy Spirit to speak to you through your study. Write down at least three lessons that you can learn from Barnabas.

- We saw how Barnabas had a very important influence for the Kingdom on these people:

1. *The Church in Antioch*
2. *Paul*
3. *John Mark*

Ask the Holy Spirit to reveal three people to you that you can encourage, comfort, and strengthen. Pray for them, invest in them and do whatever you can to help them grow in Christ.

- Take 20-30 minutes in prayer. Ask the Father to make you an encourager and comforter. Invite Him to bring the necessary transformation for that to happen. Ask for the grace to become a son of encouragement.

CLOSING WORDS

See how great a love the Father has given us, that we would be called children of God; and in fact we are. For this reason the world does not know us: because it did not know Him. Beloved, now we are children of God, and it has not appeared as yet what we will be. We know that when He appears, we will be like Him, because we will see Him just as He is. (1 John 3:1-2)

The gospel reveals that through Jesus, the Father has brought us home and restored us into our identity as sons and daughters. His motivation in doing all of this is His incredible love for us. It is by knowing His love for us that we find our true purpose. We were created to be loved by God. In this book, we have studied how this means more than just knowing that God is a Father who loves. It means living with a daily experience and revelation of Him being *my* Father who loves *me*. This is what we have been talking about throughout this book and hopefully, it has helped you to connect with the heart of God in deeper ways.

I meet a lot of frustrated believers who are wondering about their purpose and calling in life. Longing to find purpose and meaning is a good thing. After all, by knowing that God is our true Father, we also know that we haven't been created just by chance. Our Father has created us because He loves us and wants us to be in His family. This means that He wants you to know Him in a deep and personal way. I cannot think of anything that would be more exciting or meaningful than having a personal relationship with God. This is the reason for which you live and everything else in life is meant to flow out of that relationship. It is by walking with Him that we will find the purpose and meaning of our life. The gospel is that simple!

Your Notes from the Activations

If you have been doing the activations in the end of every chapter while reading this book, you have taken notes of the revelations that the Holy Spirit has provided to you. I suggest that you spend some time after you have finished this book to meditate and pray over these insights. They are the Father's gifts of love to you, His beloved and favored child. I'm confident that you'll be amazed by how much He has revealed to you through these activations. Maybe they even have provided material for you to write your own book?

The Next Book & a Final Greeting

In the next book in this series, we're picking up where this book ended. That book is called *Partnering with the Love of Christ*. It's a book on the topic of how we can partner with the love of Christ to build a dynamic relationship with Him. You were never meant to live in passivity. You have been given grace to respond to His will and build a relationship with the Father, that keeps growing deeper and more intimate. Our best days are most definitely ahead of us because Jesus always saves the best wine for last.

There is probably a lot of things that could be written as a final encouragement, but I think that the best way to end this book is by leaving you with these words: *Your Father loves you and He is well pleased with you!*

BIBLIOGRAPHY

Unless otherwise indicated, all scriptural quotations are from the *King James Version* of the Bible.

Scripture references marked AMP are taken from Amplified® Bible Copyright © 2015 by The Lockman Foundation, La Habra, CA 90631.

Scripture references marked The Message are taken from The Message. Copyright © 1993, 1994, 1995, 1996, 2000, 2001, 2002.

Scripture references marked NASB are taken from NEW AMERICAN STANDARD BIBLE® NASB® Copyright © 1960, 1971, 1977,1995, 2020 by The Lockman Foundation A Corporation Not for Profit La Habra, CA. All Rights Reserved.

Scripture references marked NIV are taken from the HOLY BIBLE, NEW INTERNATIONAL VERSION®. NIV®. Copyright © 1973, 1978, 1984 by the International Bible Society.

Scripture quotations marked NLT are taken from the Holy Bible, New Living Translation, copyright 1996, 2004, 2007, 2015 by Tyndale House Foundation. Used by permission of Tyndale House Publishers, Inc., Carol Stream, Illinois 60188. All rights reserved.

Scripture references marked NKJV are taken from The Holy Bible, New King James Version, Copyright © 1982 Thomas Nelson. All rights reserved.

Scripture references marked TPT are taken from The Passion Translation® is a registered trademark of Passion & Fire Ministries, Inc. Copyright © 2020 Passion & Fire Ministries, Inc.

ABOUT THE AUTHOR

Martin Reén lives in the north of Sweden together with His wife Linda and their three lovely children, Isak, Benjamin and Noomi. Martin's and Linda's vision has always been to get to know the heart of the Father in deeper ways, to grow in intimacy with Jesus Christ, and to be conformed into His image. Martin's vision is to introduce as many parts of the body of Christ as possible to the love of the Father and the finished work of Jesus Christ, so that the believers can become secure in their identity as sons and daughters of God and learn to live by the life of Christ. Martin and Linda travel all over the world to preach the gospel and to teach in Bible schools, seminars, conferences, and on-line events. They work with mission, counselling, and leadership training as well.